SUPER SKILLS

HOW TO PLAY GUITAR
IN 10 EASY LESSONS

DAN HOLTON

QED
QED Publishing

ABOUT THE AUTHOR

Dan Holton began playing the guitar at 15 after falling in love with the blues, and he hasn't been without a guitar since. He has toured and played in numerous bands and has a degree in Music. Dan has built up various guitar tuition businesses and is now the owner and managing director of Your Guitar Academy.

Your Guitar Academy is the central hub for the ultimate private guitar lesson experience. The company brings together experienced guitar tutors with a comprehensive range of course materials and online support. See www.yourguitaracademy.com for more information and to find a guitar academy near you.

First published in the UK in 2015 by
QED Publishing
A Quarto Group company
The Old Brewery
6 Blundell Street
London N7 9BH

www.qed-publishing.co.uk

A catalogue record for this book is available from the British Library.

ISBN: 978 1 78493 037 0 (spiral-bound edition)
ISBN: 978 1 78493 132 2 (hardback edition)

Printed in China

Publisher: Zeta Jones
Art Director: Susi Martin
Managing Editor: Laura Knowles
Design: Punch Bowl Design
Original illustrations: Joanna Kerr (throughout)
                        Nina Cosford (cover and pages 3, 19)

Picture credits: Shutterstock 3 Monkik; 7top, 56 centre, 56 bottom NEGOVURA; 8 top Elena Kazanskaya.

CONTENTS

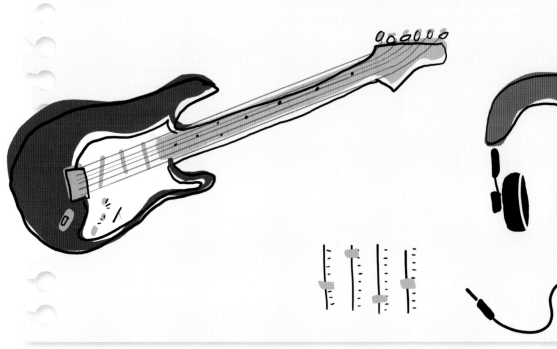

INTRODUCTION

WELCOME TO THE WORLD OF GUITAR!

Here we are at the start of your journey learning the guitar! This book will guide you through everything you need to know as a beginner guitarist in a simple, step-by-step fashion. Let's start by getting motivated! Think about what your goal is on the guitar. What's going to make you pick up the instrument every day to practise?

WHAT'S YOUR GOAL?

Do you love the sound of electric guitar and dream of playing in a rock band?

Or maybe acoustic is your thing. Does the idea of writing songs and singing on acoustic really get you excited about playing?

Perhaps you want to play in a live band one day in front of an adoring crowd. Or maybe you simply want to be able to play and sing along to a few of your favourite songs in the comfort of your own home.

Whatever your goal is, this book will help you get there! All you need to do is follow the steps exactly as they are written, and keep practicing. By the end of this short book, you will be a fully fledged guitar player with all the tools necessary to take your playing to the next level.

LOOK OUT FOR THESE AUDIO LINKS

Look out for these boxes – they will tell you when you can listen and play along to audio tracks online. All you need to do is go to www.qed-publishing.co.uk/superskillsguitaraudio and follow the links.

Step 1: WHAT YOU WILL NEED

Let's do a quick check of what you need to get started.

1. YOUR GUITAR (& AMPLIFIER)

Sounds obvious, but learning to play guitar is a very hands-on experience. You will not learn how to play by simply reading the book. Every step of the way, you need to practise very specific things, so you should have your guitar ready to go when you open the book! It doesn't matter if you use acoustic or electric at this stage.

If you do use an electric guitar, you'll need a little practice amplifier (amp). Don't spend too much money at this stage. You can always upgrade later. A digital amp with a headphone jack is a great place to start.

QUICK TIP

It's a good idea to take your guitar to a 'guitar tech' in your area. It is very likely that the guitar needs a 'set up' because the strings are too high. This makes it hard to play and can be extremely frustrating. Someone at a music shop or a local guitar tech can easily get it set up for you!

2. THE BITS & BOBS

1 PLECTRUMS You must have a few plectrums or 'picks' ready to go. These come in all shapes and sizes. Just stick with a medium-weight one (between 0.9 and 1.2 mm gauge) and you'll be fine!

2 TUNER At this stage of your guitar career, you won't be able to tune by ear, so buy an electric tuner from a music shop. Get the salesman to show you how to use it before you leave.

3 GUITAR STRAP Your guitar should come with a strap but, if not, you can pick one up from your local music shop. It will really help with holding the guitar in these early days.

3. MOTIVATION

So, you have the gear, you're excited, you're motivated... Let's get started with **Skill 1** on the next page.

GOOD LUCK!

GETTING STARTED

Let's get you comfortable with the instrument. Below details the best way to hold the guitar (both acoustic and electric). This may be uncomfortable at first, but with a few days of practice under your belt it'll feel totally natural.

ACOUSTIC GUITAR

Sit the guitar on your leg where the natural curve fits snugly. Rest your right arm on the body of the guitar so you can get your plectrum hand right by the hole of the guitar.

QUICK TIP

You should be able to let go of the neck with your left hand and keep the guitar secure with just your right arm leaning on the body.

It's a good idea to sit on a stool where you can raise your right leg higher to help keep the guitar up in position.

ELECTRIC GUITAR

Sit the body of the guitar on your right leg. Rest the guitar's natural curve on your leg. Notice how the right arm leans on the body of the guitar to keep it stable.

Wear a strap! This will help keep the guitar in a position that allows your fretting hand to reach the strings easily.

CHOOSING & HOLDING THE PICK

Throughout this book we will be using a pick, also called a plectrum, so it is very important to understand which pick to use and how to hold it properly.

1. WHICH PICK TO CHOOSE?

IT TAKES PRACTICE TO BE A PERFECT PICKER

For the time being, let's keep it simple and use a medium-gauge pick. 'Gauge' is the measurement of thickness. You should be looking for something between 0.6 and 0.85 millimetres (mm). The gauge is normally printed on the front of the pick.

2. HOW TO HOLD THE PICK

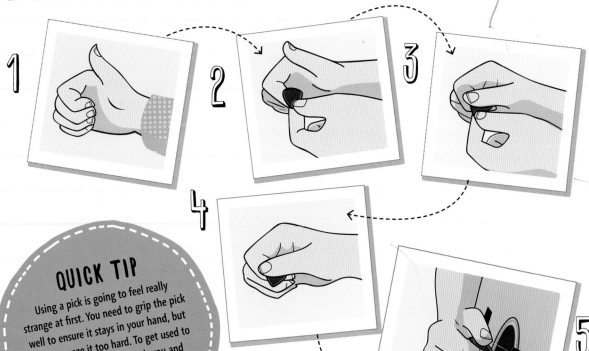

QUICK TIP

Using a pick is going to feel really strange at first. You need to grip the pick well to ensure it stays in your hand, but don't squeeze it too hard. To get used to the pick, take one out with you and practise the grip away from the guitar. This will really help.

YOUR FIRST THREE CHORDS

Chords make up the backbone of all songs. A chord is essentially two or more notes played together. To play chords, we need to know a little more about the guitar and its strings.

Part 1: GUITAR PARTS

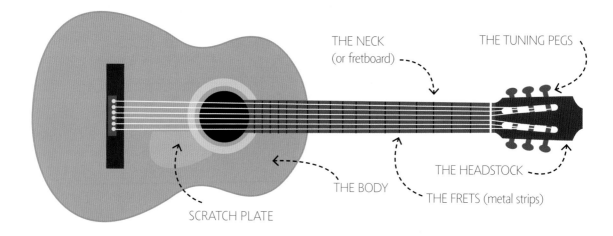

THE NECK
(or fretboard)

THE TUNING PEGS

THE BODY

THE HEADSTOCK

THE FRETS (metal strips)

SCRATCH PLATE

Part 2: GUITAR STRINGS

In order to understand most guitar-related music, we MUST know the six strings on the guitar. From low to high (thick to thin string), they are E, A, D, G, B and E.

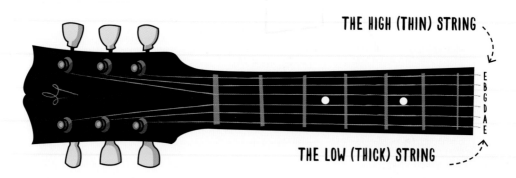

THE HIGH (THIN) STRING

E
B
G
D
A
E

THE LOW (THICK) STRING

Use this acronym to help you remember the strings, starting from the low E:

Elephants And Donkeys Grow Big Ears

Part 3: CHORD BOXES & FRETTING CHORDS PROPERLY

Now let's take a look at the chord boxes. These show us how to play any chord we are learning. You will see them everywhere on the internet and in guitar magazines. Here is our first chord, Asus2.

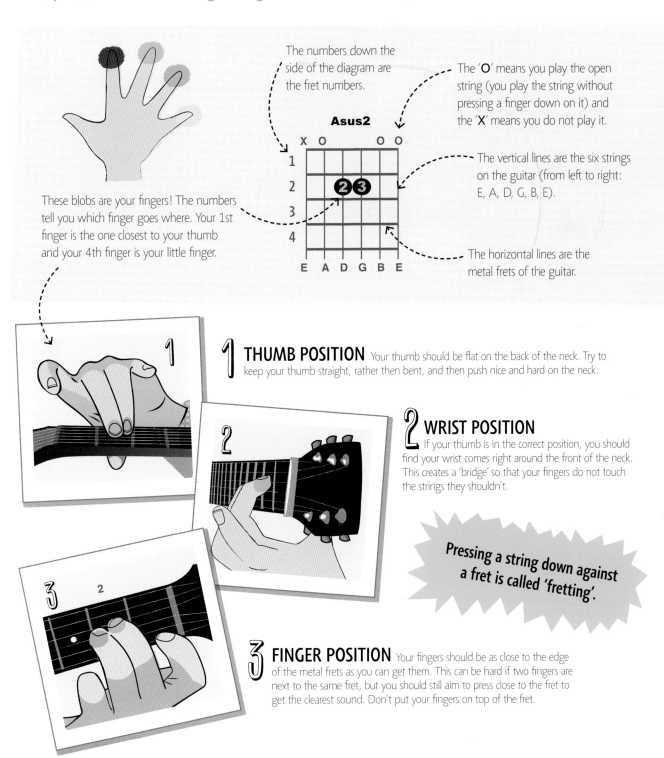

The numbers down the side of the diagram are the fret numbers.

The 'O' means you play the open string (you play the string without pressing a finger down on it) and the 'X' means you do not play it.

Asus2

The vertical lines are the six strings on the guitar (from left to right: E, A, D, G, B, E).

These blobs are your fingers! The numbers tell you which finger goes where. Your 1st finger is the one closest to your thumb and your 4th finger is your little finger.

The horizontal lines are the metal frets of the guitar.

1 THUMB POSITION Your thumb should be flat on the back of the neck. Try to keep your thumb straight, rather then bent, and then push nice and hard on the neck.

2 WRIST POSITION If your thumb is in the correct position, you should find your wrist comes right around the front of the neck. This creates a 'bridge' so that your fingers do not touch the strings they shouldn't.

Pressing a string down against a fret is called 'fretting'.

3 FINGER POSITION Your fingers should be as close to the edge of the metal frets as you can get them. This can be hard if two fingers are next to the same fret, but you should still aim to press close to the fret to get the clearest sound. Don't put your fingers on top of the fret.

Part 4: THREE CHORD SHAPES

Here are the first three chords that we need to learn. Focus on getting these chords to sound as clear as you can. Position the fingers of your left hand as shown in the diagrams and, with your right hand, pick through all six strings. Try to get each one of them to sound clearly. The strings you have your fingers on might sound a little 'buzzy'. If so, you need to push down a bit harder and move your fingers closer to the edge of the fret.

Have a listen to what these chords sound like by visiting the audio track webpage (see page 4) and clicking on the link to Skill 1 – Asus2, Cmaj7 & Em

ASUS2

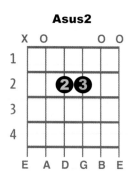

FRONT VIEW

PLAYER'S VIEW

QUICK TIP

The lower your thumb is on the back of the neck (vertically), the more your wrist will come round and the better that 'bridge' will be.

C MAJOR 7TH

QUICK TIP

This one will really stretch your middle two fingers! To make the chord clear, you need both fingers to be right up to the edge of each fret.

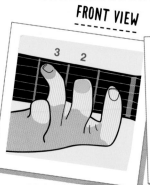

FRONT VIEW

PLAYER'S VIEW

E MINOR

FRONT VIEW

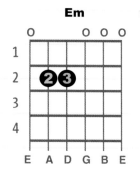

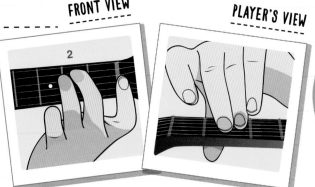

PLAYER'S VIEW

QUICK TIP

The challenge with this chord is getting the G string to ring out. It helps if you create a good bridge with your 3rd finger.

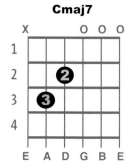

Part 5: MOVING THE CHORDS

Once you have tried all three chords, it is time to memorise them. In the world of guitar, we use the term 'muscle memory'. To fully learn the chords, you need to engage your fingers' muscle memory. To do this you need to start changing between the three chords.

1. CHANGING CHORDS

Try playing the Asus2, followed by the Cmaj7, followed by the Em. Then repeat. The focus here is *not* how clear the chord sounds. The focus is getting your fingers to simply remember the shapes and move to the shapes as quickly as you can. So, don't worry if the chords sound pretty awful sometimes. Your focus is getting to the chord shapes quickly.

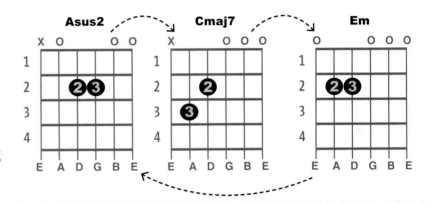

2. CHORD FOCUS

After repeating step 1 until your fingers can take no more (and they will start to hurt!), move on to Step 2. Here the focus *is* perfection. Take each chord individually and take your time fretting it until it sounds as perfect as you can get it. Your fingers will really feel it by this stage, but just a little more…

3. REPEAT

Once you have played through all three chords as perfectly as you can, it is time for a short break. This 5- to 10-minute break gives your muscle memory a chance to register what has just happened and start working. Return to the guitar after this break and start again from Step 1. You will immediately see an improvement, however slight!

BEFORE STARTING THE NEXT SKILL…

Congratulations – you've got to the end of the first skill! However, that doesn't mean you can dive straight into the next one. There are a couple of things you need to do before you move on.

1 PRACTISE
You should be able to play these three chords without looking at the book. They don't have to sound perfect yet, but you need to be able to play them without looking AND change between them. Have some fun doing it as well!

2 UNDERSTAND
Do you know the six string names off by heart? Can you read and understand the chord boxes? Are you comfortable with the pick and holding the guitar? If the answer to these questions is yes, then you're ready to move on to the next skill.

READING GUITAR TAB

Guitar tab (short for 'tablature') is a simplified music notation for guitarists. Almost all guitar music these days is written out using tab. If you're going to learn guitar, you'll need to read from guitar tab, so let's get a head start!

Step 1: THE MYSTERIOUS TAB

The vertical lines represent the end of a musical bar. In a typical song you will have four beats, then a bar line to make the whole thing easier to read.

The horizontal lines are the guitar strings. They are depicted in blue here for clarity, but will not always be.

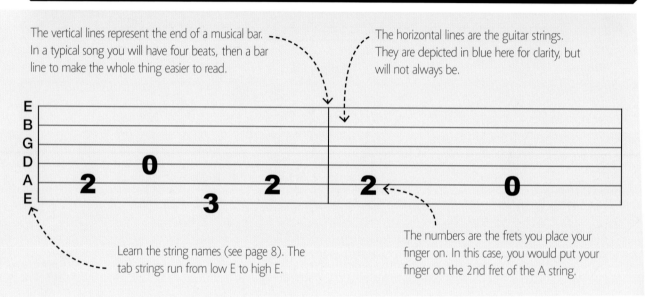

Learn the string names (see page 8). The tab strings run from low E to high E.

The numbers are the frets you place your finger on. In this case, you would put your finger on the 2nd fret of the A string.

Tab is essentially a grid based on the guitar neck. The key to understanding it is recognising that the number tells you which fret, and the horizontal line tells you which string.

Looking at the neck of the guitar should make it easier to see how the tab is read. Get to grips with the string names and the fret order before moving on.

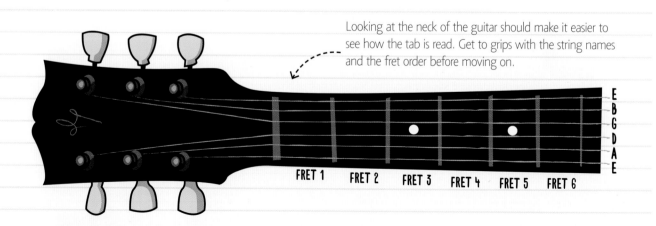

Step 2: WHICH FINGERS?!

Tab shows us where our fingers need to be on the fretboard, which is a very good start! However, traditional tab does not tell you which fingers to use when you fret the note, which can be confusing. If the tab says,

'Play the 2nd fret on the A string', this doesn't mean you have to use your 2nd finger! So, to make things clearer, we will now introduce four colours, each indicating a different finger.

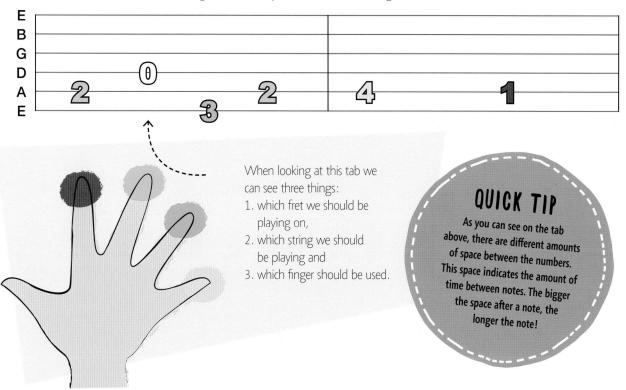

When looking at this tab we can see three things:
1. which fret we should be playing on,
2. which string we should be playing and
3. which finger should be used.

QUICK TIP

As you can see on the tab above, there are different amounts of space between the numbers. This space indicates the amount of time between notes. The bigger the space after a note, the longer the note!

Step 3: THE THOUGHT PROCESS

Just in case you haven't quite picked up the concept of tab, here is the process in slow motion.

1 The first number is blue, it's the number 2 and it's on the A string. This tells you that you need to put your second finger (blue) onto the 2nd fret of the A string and play the note.

2 The next number along is white, it's 0 and it's on the D string. '0' means no fret. Therefore you simply play the open D string without putting any fingers down.

3 The third number along is green, it's the number 3 and it's on the E string. So, you take your third finger and play the 3rd fret of the E string.

4 The fourth number along is blue, it's the number 2 and it's on the A string. This is exactly the same as the first note. The bar line tells us we are moving into the next bar. Carry on playing the two notes in the next bar in the same way.

SPIDER EXERCISES

The time has come to put your tab reading skills into practice! We will be looking at two 'spider exercises'. These exercises are great for getting your left and right hand synchronised. Focus on making each of your four fingers work individually. So, when your brain says 'I need to lift my third finger', that's exactly what you do. The first exercise is called '5,6,7,8'.

Exercise 1: 5,6,7,8 SPIDER

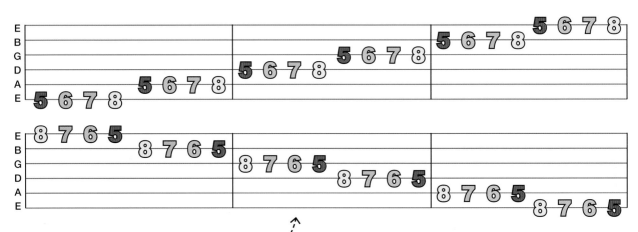

Looking over the tab, you will soon spot the pattern. You put one finger in front of the other as you crawl up or down the fretboard. Remember to use the correct fingers, as shown below.

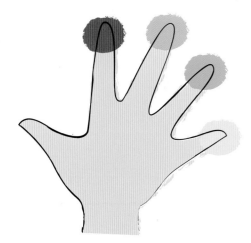

THE CORRECT HAND POSITION

Make sure your thumb is straight and pressed on the back of the neck so your fingers will be able to stretch across four frets. Try to place the thumb flat in the same position you see here in the picture. Do not let that thumb joint bend!

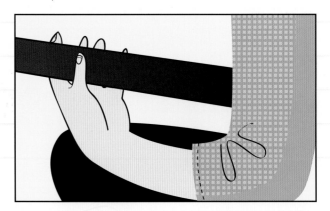

WALK-THROUGH

Let's quickly walk through this exercise. Begin by getting your fingers in the right position. They need to be stretched out across all four frets before you even start. This will force you to find the correct hand and wrist position, with the thumb at the back of the neck.

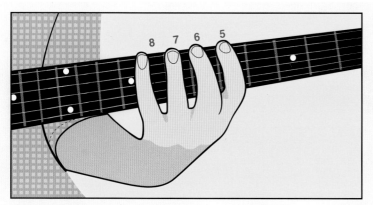

HAND POSITION

Here is how you should position your wrist. Notice that the thumb is at the back of the neck and all four fingers can stretch across the correct frets. So the 1st finger is on the 5th fret, and the 4th finger is on the 8th fret. Be sure to have this position correct before starting.

FRONT VIEW

BACK VIEW

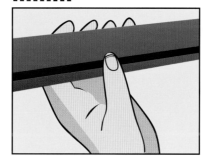

PLAYER'S VIEW

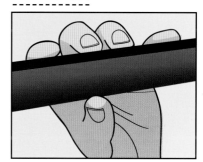

Now off you go! Keep the correct hand position as you continue through the notes. Play the 5th fret, then 6th, then 7th, then 8th. Then get to the A string by moving the hand position down one string. Continue to do that each time. Then do the whole thing in reverse on the way back!

1 HALF WAY DOWN THE EXERCISE

2 AT THE BOTTOM STRING

3 ON THE WAY BACK!

ALTERNATE PICKING

Alternate picking simply means that you pick down and up on a single string. This action will make it a lot easier to play the exercise in the long run. Do it correctly from the start and in a few weeks you'll be glad you did!

WALK-THROUGH

1 DOWNSTROKE

When you start the 5,6,7,8 exercise, the first pick stroke should be a downstroke on the 5th fret E string (the first note).

2 UPSTROKE

You should then pick the next note, which will be the 6th fret E string, with an upstroke. When you play the third note (7th fret E string), do a downstroke again. Continue to alternate between the two as you play each note of the exercise.

PICK POSITION

Try to lean the ball of your thumb on the bridge of the guitar (see page 6) when using the plectrum.

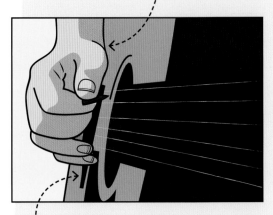

Some players like to secure the picking hand by placing the little finger on the scratch plate, as shown here. This is optional, but give it a try if you are struggling to pick accurately.

USING A METRONOME

When you first start playing the spider exercise on the previous page, it may very well seem impossible. Don't worry! This feeling happens a lot when playing the guitar, but within a few weeks you will wonder how you ever thought you couldn't play it. To truly master this exercise, you should be using a metronome or drum loop. The speed of a piece of music is measured in something called BPM (beats per minute), and we will start at 70 BPM.

Listen online to what Exercise 1 and 2 should sound like. They are played against a drum loop set at 70 BPM. Your aim is to be able to play along with these tracks at this speed. This is a hard task, so take your time and keep trying!

1 Skill 2 – 5,6,7,8 Spider Exercise

2 Skill 2 – 5,7,6,8 Spider Exercise

3 Skill 2 – 5-Minute DRUM LOOP

This is a long repeating drum loop set to 70 BPM. Once you can play along to the first two tracks, try playing along to this one for as long as possible.

Exercise 2: 5,7,6,8 SPIDER

The second spider exercise is a little trickier than 5,6,7,8, so only tackle it after a week or so of getting the first exercise together. Here is the tab.

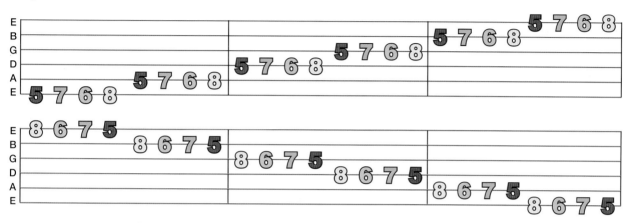

Just as before, focus on which fingers play which frets, as this is a key part of the exercise. Remember to keep your thumb at the back of the neck and gradually move through the exercise whilst trying to keep a really good hand position. Your thumb should move down the back of the neck with you as you play through all the strings. As mentioned above, this exercise is quite a bit harder than the previous one, so don't worry if you really struggle. Remember to alternate pick the entire exercise as well!

BEFORE STARTING THE NEXT SKILL...

Congratulations for getting to the end of Skill 2! However, these exercises do not end here. They should now become your guitar warm-up. Every time you pick up the guitar to play, you should spend 5 or 10 minutes running through both of these exercises. At first, playing them for 5 minutes will seriously ache, so only do as much as you can. As your hand gets stronger, try to push yourself and get to 10 minutes. Your practice routine should look a little like the one on the right.

1 WARM-UPS Run through the 5,6,7,8 and 5,7,6,8 spider exercises. First do them without the audio, then add the drum loops to push you harder. Do the warm-ups for 5–10 minutes and log your speed. Try to play it a little faster every week.

2 OPEN CHORDS Move on to open chord practice for the rest of your practice session. This was outlined in the last chapter. Try to practise these for 10–20 minutes at a time.

Once you have used this practice routine for a week or so, it is time to move on to the next skill. Give yourself a pat on the back for a good job so far, and let's begin learning your first song!

YOUR FIRST SONG

In this chapter you will apply everything you have learnt so far by learning how to play a whole song. This song consists of a riff (see page 21) which has been tabbed out for you, as well as a full chord chart to play along to.

NOW IT'S GETTING REALLY EXCITING!

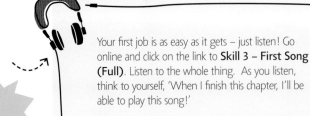

Your first job is as easy as it gets – just listen! Go online and click on the link to **Skill 3 – First Song (Full)**. Listen to the whole thing. As you listen, think to yourself, 'When I finish this chapter, I'll be able to play this song!'

Step 1: READING CHORD CHARTS

A chord chart is a basic outline of the song in chords. It tells you which chords to play in the song and how long to play each chord for. It doesn't give you any finer details than that. It won't tell you how to play the lead guitar part or what rhythms to play, just the chords.

A SAMPLE CHORD CHART

This is the chord you should be playing (Asus2). The diagonal lines basically say 'continue playing that chord'.

The diagonal lines are the beats of the bar. So these four diagonal lines show four beats, which make up one bar.

VERSE

Asus2 /// //// **Cmaj7** /// ////
Asus2 /// //// **Cmaj7** /// ////

When you see three diagonal lines, it's because the chord counts as the first beat. So it's 'Asus2, 2, 3, 4'.

CHORUS

Asus2 /// **Em** /// **Asus2** /// **Em** ///

The chord chart will tell you when you are in the chorus, verse, intro or outro.

Still unsure? Visit the **Skill 3 – Chord Chart** link to hear how the chord chart is played.

PLAYING THE CHORD CHART

Look at the chord chart on page 18. First, we start with the verse. Play Asus2 for two bars (out loud, you could say, 'Asus2, 2, 3, 4 – 1, 2, 3, 4'). Then play Cmaj7 for two bars. Then do exactly the same thing again; play Asus2 for another two bars and Cmaj7 for another two bars. Next, move on to the chorus. Play Asus2 for one bar, Em for one bar, Asus2 for one bar and then Em for a final bar. That's it!

$step$ 2: **READING TAB**

Another big factor in learning to play this song is reading the lead part from the tab. Let's have a quick recap of how to read tab.

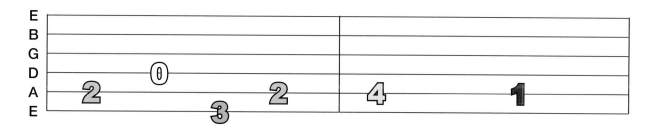

TAB RECAP

1 LINES
The horizontal lines are the strings, whilst the vertical lines indicate the bars (four beats).

2 NUMBERS
The numbers represent which fret you put your fingers on. So the first number (2) tells you to play the 2nd fret of the A string.

3 COLOURS
The colours tell you which finger to use for which notes. See the colour-code hand to the right!

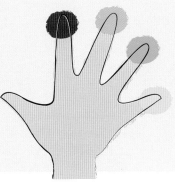

THE CHORD CHART FOR YOUR FIRST SONG

Now that we have the basics covered, let's look at the chord chart for this song.

You will not be playing these chords during the intro, you will be playing the riff that you will learn on page 21. However, these are the chords underneath the riff.

INTRO (RIFF)

Asus2 /// **Cmaj7** /// **Asus2** /// **Cmaj7** ///
Asus2 /// **Cmaj7** /// **Asus2** /// **Cmaj7** ///

VERSE

Asus2 /// **Cmaj7** /// **Asus2** /// **Cmaj7** ///
Asus2 /// **Cmaj7** /// **Asus2** /// **Cmaj7** ///
Asus2 /// **Cmaj7** /// **Asus2** /// **Cmaj7** ///
Asus2 /// **Cmaj7** /// **Asus2** /// **Cmaj7** ///

You then switch to strumming the chords in the verse (see page 24). It is only one strum on each chord. As you can see, the chords last for one bar each. So you say, 'Strum, 2, 3, 4 – Strum, 2, 3, 4'.

CHORUS

Em / **Cmaj7** / **Asus2** / **Cmaj7** /
Em / **Cmaj7** / **Asus2** / **Cmaj7** /
Em / **Cmaj7** / **Asus2** / **Cmaj7** /
Em / **Cmaj7** / **Asus2** / **Cmaj7** /
Em /// ////

(REPEAT TWO MORE TIMES)

In the chorus, play each chord for half a bar, which is 2 beats. So you say, 'Strum, 2, strum, 4 – Strum, 2, strum, 4'. This is challenging because the chords move quickly!

When you get to the end of the chart, repeat it two more times to complete the song.

Step 3: PLAY THE CHORD CHART

Spend a few minutes getting familiar with the chord chart on the previous page. When you think you have the changes memorised, it's time to return to the online audio tracks.

The full song you listened to can wait for the moment. Instead, click on the link to **Skill 3 – First Song (Guitar Loud)** to hear a version of the song that has the strummed guitar very loud. This will make it clear what you should be playing along with, so put it on and play along!

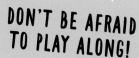

DON'T BE AFRAID TO PLAY ALONG!

Step 4: THE RIFF TAB

The next thing to learn is the riff. A riff is a repeated melody within a piece of music that is often a very recognisable part of the song. We will start by letting you work out how to play it based on the tab. We'll go into it in more detail on the next page, but before you jump into the full walk-through, why not give it a go by yourself?

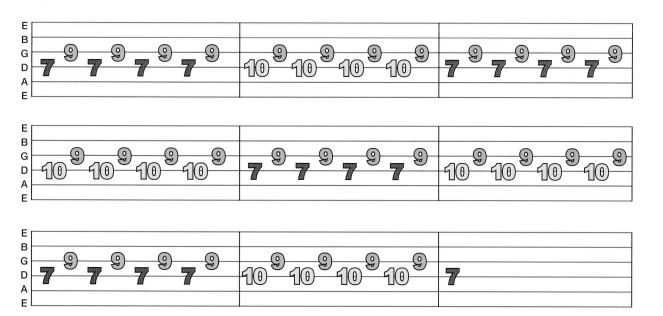

RIFF WALK-THROUGH

The tab of the song essentially shows a loop of the first two bars. Let's look at these two bars in a little more detail.

For the first bar, place your fingers on the guitar as if you were playing a chord. See how the 1st and 3rd fingers are on the correct frets. The plectrum hand simply picks between them.

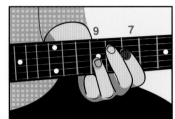

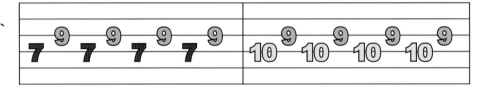

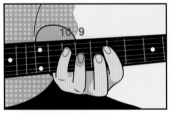

It's the same principle with the second bar. You simply keep the 3rd finger where it is on the 9th fret and then add the 4th finger to the 10th fret D string. This can be a little tricky as the little finger often doesn't want to push down very hard. Be sure it doesn't accidentally muffle the G string as well. (Create that bridge we talked about in Skill 1!)

THUMB POSITION

As you play this riff for four bars, you need to make sure your thumb is in a good position to ensure you are able to keep pressure on the strings the entire time. This is going to challenge your hand strength. If it really hurts (and starts to shake), then it's time to stop.

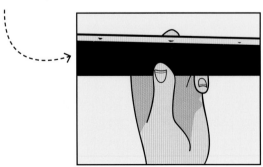

ALTERNATE PICKING!

Don't forget to do down–up strokes when picking. For example, when playing the first four notes, the 7 should be a down stroke, 9 an up, 7 down, 9 up. Continue like this all the way through.

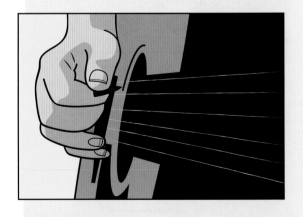

Step 5: PUTTING IT ALL TOGETHER

When you are able to play the tab, it's time to try it with the full song. We are also going to try and play the entire song (including the chords). This means that you need to play the entire riff, then jump straight to the Asus2 chord for the start of the verse.

Time to return to that main song, except let's try it without the vocals first. This will help you to concentrate on the guitar parts you are playing, and not on the lovely singing! Click on the link to **Skill 3 – First Song (No Vocals).**

RIFF FOR THE INTRO

```
7  7  7  7  7  9 |10  9 10  9 10  9 | 7  7  7  7  7  9

10  9 10  9 10  9 | 7  7  7  7  7  9 |10  9 10  9 10  9

7  7  7  7  7  9 |10  9 10  9 10  9 | 7
```

CHORDS FOR THE VERSE AND CHORUS

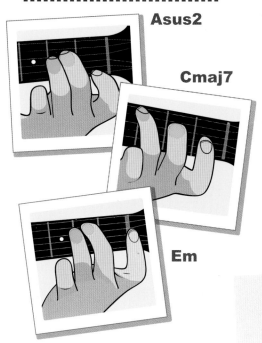

Asus2

Cmaj7

Em

INTRO (RIFF)
Asus2 /// **Cmaj7** /// **Asus2** /// **Cmaj7** ///
Asus2 /// **Cmaj7** /// **Asus2** /// **Cmaj7** ///

VERSE
Asus2 /// **Cmaj7** /// **Asus2** /// **Cmaj7** ///
Asus2 /// **Cmaj7** /// **Asus2** /// **Cmaj7** ///
Asus2 /// **Cmaj7** /// **Asus2** /// **Cmaj7** ///
Asus2 /// **Cmaj7** /// **Asus2** /// **Cmaj7** ///

CHORUS
Em / **Cmaj7** / **Asus2** / **Cmaj7** /
Em / **Cmaj7** / **Asus2** / **Cmaj7** /
Em / **Cmaj7** / **Asus2** / **Cmaj7** /
Em / **Cmaj7** / **Asus2** / **Cmaj7** /
Em /// ////

(REPEAT TWO MORE TIMES)

When you are comfortable with the stripped-down song, return to the audio track of the full song and play along to the vocals. Have some fun doing it! Once you've done that, we'll see you in the next chapter.

INJECTING SOME RHYTHM

It's time to learn how to play some rhythm guitar. In this chapter, we will focus on learning how to use rhythm patterns and tackle the 'universal rhythm pattern'. Then we will put it into practice straightaway using our chord shapes. Let's start by asking the basic question...

...WHAT IS A RHYTHM PATTERN?

The easiest way to answer this question is by explaining how your basic song is made up. In general, we have three elements:

1 CHORD CHART
As we saw in the last chapter, a song is made up of a selection of chords in a certain order.

2 THE MELODY
This can be a singer's vocal line or a guitarist's riff, for example. The melody relies on the chord selection and sits on top of it in the music.

3 THE RHYTHM
This is the 'groove' of the song, the thing that makes you either get up and dance or sit and listen. Depending on the genre of music, the rhythm can be supplied by drums, guitar, bass or even just clapping!

Guitar rhythm patterns are a way to show the rhythm on paper. The rhythm pattern can turn a very normal, standard song (chord chart and melody) into something far more exciting and interesting to listen to.

STRUMMING PATTERN

Rhythm patterns on the guitar are also known as strumming patterns. 'Strumming' is the term used when we run the plectrum across all the strings. Pick up your guitar. Using your plectrum, strum all the strings down and then up. Keep doing this until you are essentially just going down, up, down, up over and over again. This is a strumming pattern. It's a simple one, but you are strumming! Let's now have a look at how to read strumming patterns.

step 1: THE BASIC STRUMMING GRID

We typically count four beats to a bar of music ('1, 2, 3, 4'), and then the next bar starts. In this case, we count this as '1 and 2 and 3 and 4 and'. This breaks our bar of four beats into eight quicker movements, '1 + 2 + 3 + 4 +'.

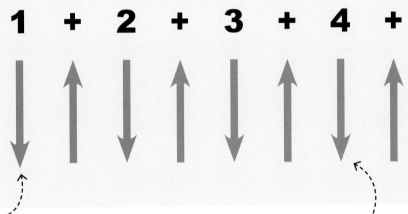

The arrows show your strumming arm movement: the down arrows show when you swing your arm downwards, and the up arrows show when you swing your arm upwards.

If an arrow is grey, it means that you should move your arm down or up, keeping the beat, but you shouldn't actually hit the strings. Basically, this is 'air strumming'.

WHICH LOOKS SOMETHING LIKE THIS...

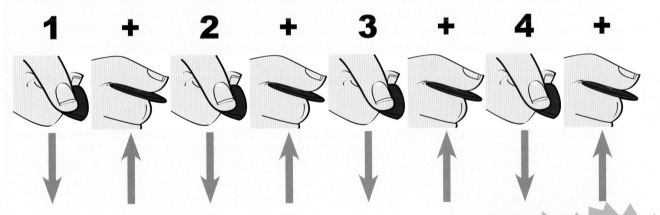

Pick up your guitar and try to do this. Your aim is to count along with your strumming. You should be counting '1' as you do your first down stroke, then 'and' as you do an upstroke, then '2' as you do the next down stroke... and so on. Look at the arrows as you do it so your brain links up with what appears on the page.

REMEMBER TO STRUM USING YOUR ARM, NOT JUST YOUR HAND – MOVE FROM YOUR ELBOW, NOT YOUR WRIST.

Step 2: ADDING THE RED ARROWS

Once you have your arm moving fluidly and can count through the strumming pattern, it is time to actually strum the guitar. A red arrow on the pattern shows when to strum the strings with the plectrum.

RHYTHM 1

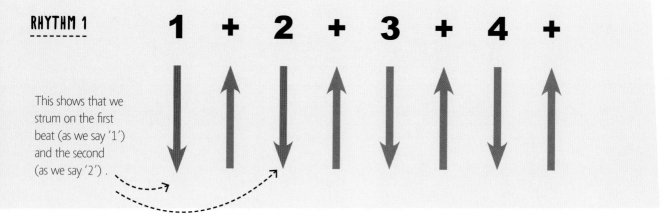

This shows that we strum on the first beat (as we say '1') and the second (as we say '2') .

WALK-THROUGH

In practice, the above rhythm pattern sounds like this:

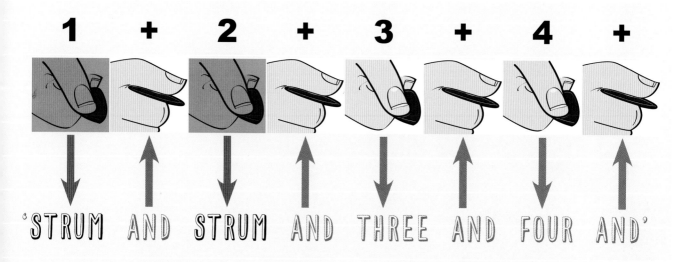

'STRUM AND STRUM AND THREE AND FOUR AND'

Go online and click on **Skill 4 – Rhythm 1**. Have a listen to this rhythm pattern and try to play along for the entire track.

Step 3: ADDING THE UPSTROKE

Let's take the strumming pattern to the next level, with the first upstroke. Be warned: this may seem simple, but it is often trickier in practice.

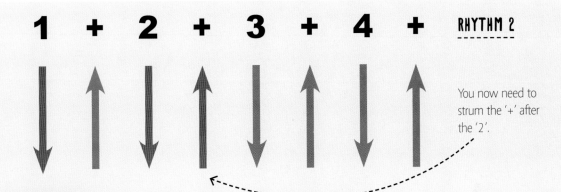

RHYTHM 2

You now need to strum the '+' after the '2'.

QUICK TIP

Once you have your arm swinging (as we did in Step 1) you never need to change that movement. You now simply need to hit the strings as you move. The more you practise, the easier it will become.

TAKE YOUR TIME & DO IT SLOWLY!

The slower you play through this rhythm pattern now, the better it will be and the quicker you will learn it. Once you get the hang of it, you won't need to constantly say, '1 and 2 and...' out loud, so don't worry! Once you have this basic pattern learnt, turn over for the universal rhythm pattern.

Click on the link to **Skill 4 – Rhythm 2**. Have a listen to this rhythm and try to play along, just as before.

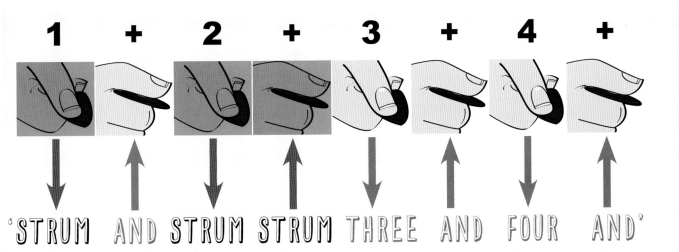

'STRUM   AND   STRUM   STRUM   THREE   AND   FOUR   AND'

THE UNIVERSAL RHYTHM PATTERN

Here we have it, the universal rhythm pattern! It is called 'universal' because it tends to work with 99 per cent of all the pop, rock and folk songs that have ever been recorded. It is also the exact pattern used on a lot of them as well. We will focus on mastering this pattern throughout the rest of the book.

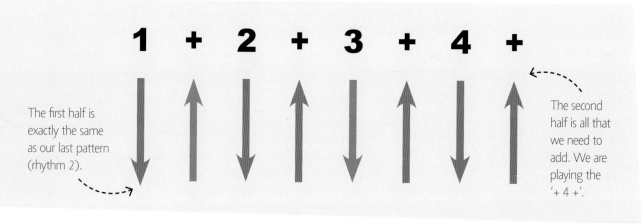

The first half is exactly the same as our last pattern (rhythm 2).

The second half is all that we need to add. We are playing the '+ 4 +'.

WHICH WILL LOOK SOMETHING LIKE...

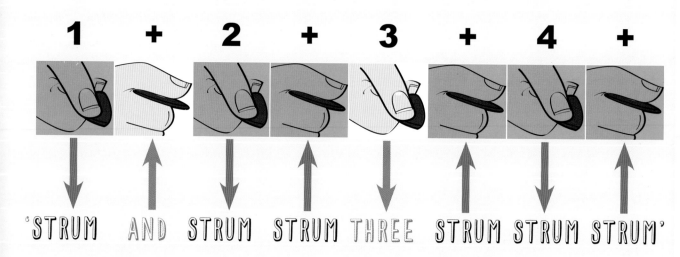

'STRUM   AND   STRUM   STRUM   THREE   STRUM   STRUM   STRUM'

Listen to the full rhythm pattern (**Skill 4 – Universal Rhythm Pattern**) and try to play along. As with all the previous patterns, there is no chord being played, just the open strings. This is so that you can focus entirely on the rhythm.

Exercise 1: ADDING CHORD CHANGES

Once you have a fair grasp of the universal rhythm pattern, let's add one of the chords to the mix. Soon you'll be strumming a rhythm and changing between a few chords. You'll be amazed how quickly this will start sounding like you're playing a song!

THE CHORD CHART

Asus2 /// //// Cmaj7 /// ////

(See page 18 to remind yourself how to read chord charts)

THE RHYTHM PATTERN (UNIVERSAL PATTERN)

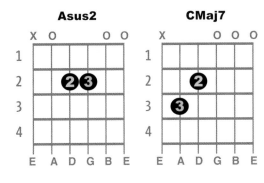

CHORD BOXES

Check your finger positions:

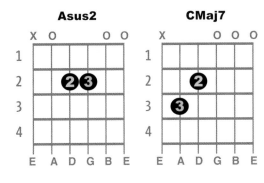

When you are ready, try to play along with **Skill 4 – Universal Rhythm Pattern (5-minute loop)**. This track loops for 5 minutes to give you plenty of practise.

Remember that the strumming pattern covers one bar (four beats). So when we combine the chord chart shown above with the universal strumming pattern, we play the pattern twice on the Asus2 (two bars) and then twice on the Cmaj7 (two bars). This chord chart will then loop round and round for as long as you can play.

STRUM-N-HUM

BEFORE MOVING ON...

Learning how to strum is a huge milestone, so don't rush it! Take your time with this and do not move on to the next skill until you can play the chord chart above whilst strumming. If you want to mix it up a bit, try choosing different chords to strum with. Maybe throw in the Em, or try to change chords every bar rather than every other bar. These are ways you can make the exercise harder, but before you attempt them, you need to focus on getting the first exercise nailed. Good luck, and when you're ready, we'll see you in the next chapter!

CHORDS, CHORDS, CHORDS!

It is time to expand your chord repertoire. In this chapter, you will be learning five new chord shapes. You will be amazed just how many popular songs you can play with these new chords, plus the three you have already learnt. It is therefore extremely important that we focus very hard on memorising and playing these new chords properly.

THE A MAJOR CHORD

A Major

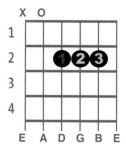

The first new chord is called A major. This chord should sound bright and happy (as do most major chords). You play five strings, from A to E. You do not play the low E string.

FRONT VIEW

PLAYER'S VIEW

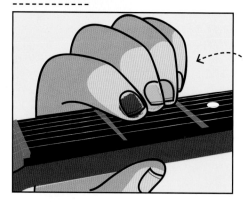

SIDE VIEW

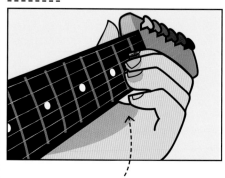

Notice that all three fingers are squeezed into one fret. Also, look at where the joints are bent to create a 'bridge' that stops the fingers from touching the strings they shouldn't.

As you have three fingers in one fret, they can't all be near the edge of it. Therefore, put the 3rd finger right on the edge of the fret, the 2nd slightly back, and the 1st further back. You may need to push down harder with the 1st finger as it is so far back from the edge of the fret.

Have a listen to what these chords should sound like. Go online and click on the link to **Skill 5 – Chords**.

THINGS TO REMEMBER

1 PUSH HARD
This chord will not come easy when you first try it. You need to put a lot of energy into pushing down the strings (especially your 1st finger). When you lift your fingers off the strings after playing the chord, you should have big dents in your fingertips!

2 THUMB
The thumb should be nice and flat at the back of the neck. This allows you to get a good hand position to create a bridge with the fingers. It is also where a lot of the pressure comes from when you push down. Try to push the thumb through the neck!

3 THE BURN
This will hurt a little! Part of learning to play new chords is realising how much strength you initially need to use. It is the same as trying to lift a heavy weight – the more you do it, the easier it becomes. This chord will feel easy in a few weeks if you feel the burn now!

THE E MAJOR CHORD

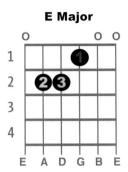

E Major

FRONT VIEW

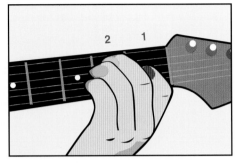

SIDE VIEW

PLAYER'S VIEW

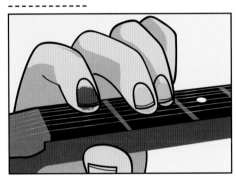

The E major chord is exactly the same as the E minor except you add your 1st finger to the G string 1st fret. Remember to position your thumb and wrist to create a bridge and get the fingers to the edge of the fret.

THE D MAJOR CHORD

D Major

FRONT VIEW

SIDE VIEW

PLAYER'S VIEW

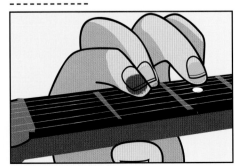

You only play four strings for the D major chord (D, G, B and E). It is a good idea to place your 1st and 2nd fingers down first and then place the 3rd finger, as it can feel like a big stretch.

QUICK TIP

Beginning guitar students find it very hard to play the high E string clearly on their first try (where your 2nd finger is). This is because the 3rd finger slightly blocks the string below. Just keep adjusting the position over a few weeks and you'll get there!

THE G MAJOR CHORD

G Major

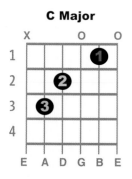

FRONT VIEW

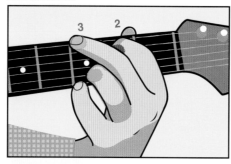

SIDE VIEW

This chord uses all of your fingers! In some ways, it's a chord of two halves: the 1st and 2nd finger on the low strings, and the 3rd and 4th on the high strings. When forming the chord, put your 3rd and 4th fingers on first.

PLAYER'S VIEW

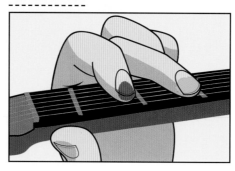

QUICK TIP

This is a tricky chord to master, so don't be too hard on yourself. The main strings to focus on getting a clear sound out of are the strings you are actually putting your fingers on. The other strings (open strings) will gradually get there!

THE C MAJOR CHORD

C Major

FRONT VIEW

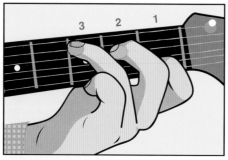

SIDE VIEW

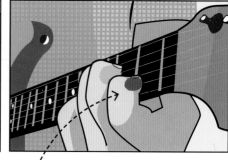

This can be the hardest open chord to get clear. You have to learn to stretch those fingers out across three frets and still get the bridge right. As with G major, practice is the only way!

PLAYER'S VIEW

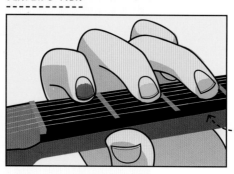

Notice how the joint at the top of the finger is totally bent. This allows you to create a bridge with the fingers even with the big finger stretch that we have in this chord.

The fingers are all at the edge of the frets for a clear sound, and the fingertips are digging into the strings to allow that bridge.

ALTERNATIVE HAND POSITION

A lot of students quickly get comfortable with the thumb at the back of the neck when playing chords, but there are a few who never quite grasp it. For those among you who just can't get comfortable in this position, there is an alternative position, with the thumb over the neck. A quick word of warning, however: this technique doesn't really work if you have small hands!

D MAJOR (ALTERNATIVE HAND POSITION)

Using D major as an example, you can see that instead of the thumb being at the back of the neck, it is over the top, wrapped around.

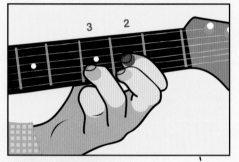

THUMB AT BACK

THUMB OVER THE NECK

BONUS!
The immediate benefit of using this hand position is that your thumb will automatically block off those low strings that you do not want ringing out. You don't need to push down with your thumb at all, just having it there will automatically deaden the string and stop it sounding.

It can be hard to choose between the two hand positions at this point, so here is a list to help you decide.

1 COMFORT
Which way do you find the most comfortable for your hand? They will both strain a bit, but which way feels easier to you?

2 CLARITY
Which way makes the chord sound clearer? This is of huge importance if you found the first way more comfortable but the chord sounded awful!

3 CHANGING
Which way makes it easier to change chords? Try moving between all the chords you know in both hand positions and decide which is easiest.

Exercise 1: PRACTISE THESE CHORDS

Based on the answers to these questions, choose one hand position and stick with it. Don't worry, though, you will be able to change it in the future if you want to. It's really just a decision for the short term. Once you have chosen, practise these three chords for a few days before you carry on to the next page of the book. Take your time. Be sure you have them memorised before tackling the next two chords. You should practise changing between the three new chords (E, A and D) and the three older ones (Asus2, Cmaj7 and Em). Have fun!

SONG TIME!

Now it's time to try a cool little acoustic-style song using the five new chords you have learnt. This is a great way to put the new chord shapes into practice. The sooner you can apply them to a song, whether it's something you have written or a song you love listening to, the sooner you will master new chord shapes. So, let's run through the song.

Your first job, as with all new songs, is to listen. Click on the link to **Skill 5 – Chord Song**. See if you can hear the main chords and the rhythm running through the song. As with all pop songs, the track is made of many layers, so try to focus only on the bit you need.

Step 1: THE CHORD CHART

The verse chords should be easy to remember, but they will be hard to play. The change between G and C is especially hard, so don't beat yourself up if this takes a while to master.

VERSE

D / / / / / / / **G** / / / **C** / / / **D** / / / / / / / **G** / / / **C** / / /
D / / / / / / / **G** / / / **C** / / / **D** / / / / / / / **G** / / / **C** / / /
D / / / / / / / **G** / / / **C** / / / **D** / / / / / / / **G** / / / **C** / / /
D / / / / / / / **G** / / / **C** / / / **D** / / / / / / / **G** / / / **C** / / /

CHORUS

E / / / **D** / / / **A** / / / / / / / **E** / / / **D** / / / **A** / / / / / /
E / / / **D** / / / **A** / / / / / / / **E** / / / **D** / / / **A** / / / / / /

The chorus is a little easier to play than the verse, but by the time you get to this section you may find your fingers feel as though they want to fall off! Keep going for as long as you can. You are training your wrist as well as your brain!

(REPEAT ONE MORE TIME)

Step 2: THE RHYTHM PATTERN

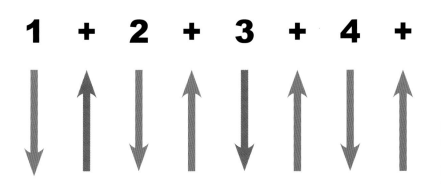

The strumming during this song is the universal rhythm pattern, so if you haven't practised it much, now is the time! You may need to practise changing chords without strumming before adding this rhythm pattern.

This song can be difficult for beginners to play. There are a lot of tricky chord changes here, so don't be discouraged if it takes a while to get them up to the speed of this track. You can listen to a stripped-down version of the track, which makes it easier to hear exactly what you should be playing. Go to **Skill 5 – Chord Song (Simple Version)**.

BEFORE YOU MOVE ON...

We are now halfway through the book. Everything steps up a gear from here on in, so it is crucial that you feel fairly confident of your skills so far. Here are some useful pointers to help you see if you're ready to move on to Skill 6.

1 CAN YOU PLAY THIS SONG?

This may sound obvious, but do not move on until you can play through this song. It doesn't have to be perfect – nowhere near perfect, in fact – but you do need to be able to just about get through the whole song without stopping. If you can do that, it means you have a good handle on rhythm and chord changes and you have some strength in your fingers and your wrist.

2 ARE YOU COMFORTABLE WITH RHYTHM?

We have now used the universal rhythm pattern in a whole song, so you should feel pretty comfortable with it. If not, you need to work on that separately until you have it right. From Skill 6 onwards, it will be assumed you can play the universal pattern easily, so make sure you can!

3 SPIDER EXERCISES

Remember your spider exercises! (You learnt them back in Chapter 2.) These will be crucial when it comes to tackling the riffs and solos we will be looking at in the second half of the book. Spider exercises are a great warm-up that you should never stop doing. Even professional guitar players use them every day.

AND THAT'S IT!
IF YOU CAN HAPPILY TICK OFF ALL OF THESE THINGS THEN LET'S GET CRACKING ON SKILL 6!

POWER CHORDS

This will be our first step away from the open position chords, as we move further up the neck. The open chords (all of the previous chords we have learnt) are great for big acoustic sounds, but not so good for electric distorted sounds. This is where power chords come in! Before we learn how to play them, we should understand how they differ from the major and minor chords. We need to start with the notes on the neck.

NOTES ON THE E STRING

The **12th fret** is where we reach the end of all the notes available and start all over again from E. There are normally two dots on this fret to show you it's the 12th.

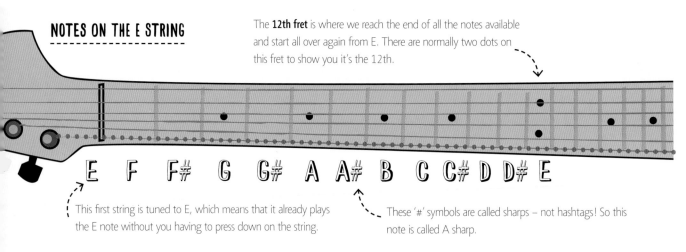

E   F   F#   G   G#   A   A#   B   C   C#   D   D#   E

This first string is tuned to E, which means that it already plays the E note without you having to press down on the string.

These '#' symbols are called sharps – not hashtags! So this note is called A sharp.

Take the E string (1st string) and climb up fret by fret, calling out the note. The first three are shown for you here. Carry on all the way to the 12th fret.

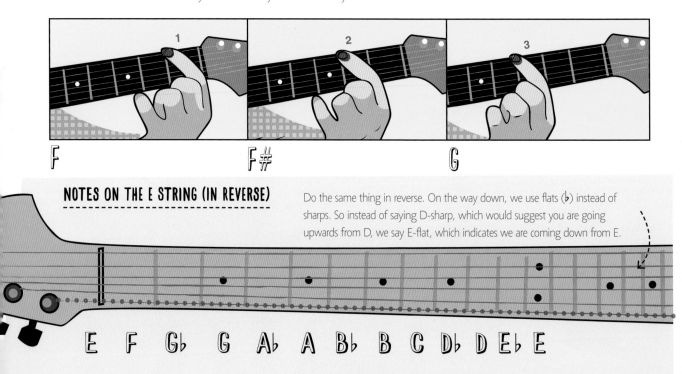

F   F#   G

NOTES ON THE E STRING (IN REVERSE)

Do the same thing in reverse. On the way down, we use flats (♭) instead of sharps. So instead of saying D-sharp, which would suggest you are going upwards from D, we say E-flat, which indicates we are coming down from E.

E   F   G♭   G   A♭   A   B♭   B   C   D♭   D   E♭   E

BASIC THEORY BEHIND CHORDS (A MUST READ!)

It's time to use our new note knowledge! Every single chord is built from something called the major scale. The major scale is 'do re mi fa so la ti do' as in the classic song from *The Sound of Music*. All of the chord shapes that we have learnt and will be learning are built from those seven notes. As an example, here is a C major scale:

1 2 3 4 5 6 7 8

C D E F G A B C

do re mi fa so la ti do

The scale returns to C on the eighth note and loops around the same seven notes again.

QUICK TIP

This theory stuff takes a while (and a lot of application) to sink in, so don't spend hours trying to understand right away. Just accept it as fact for the moment. The reasons behind it all can come later on in your guitar journey.

For any C chords that we build (C major, C minor, C major 7th and so on), you need to know the C major scale. If we were building D chords, you would need the D major scale, and so on throughout the notes. Let's stick with C for demonstration purposes and see how these major and minor chords are built. This is the point where you need your 'chord formulas'.

MAJOR CHORDS

To construct a major chord, you take these notes from the major scale:

1ST, 3RD & 5TH NOTES

Therefore, from the C major scale written above, you get the notes:

C, E & G

And there is your C major chord. You can repeat these notes as many times as you like in the chord, but you use only these three notes.

MINOR CHORDS

To construct a minor chord, you take these notes from the scale:

1ST, FLAT 3RD & 5TH NOTES

A 'flat 3rd' means you take the 3rd note and drop down one (see the guitar neck on the previous page). This gives us:

C, E♭ & G

And there you have your C minor chord! Put those notes together anywhere on the neck and you have a C minor chord.

You can see that there is a subtle difference between a major and minor chord. One slightly different note makes a world of difference to the way the music sounds. To a listener, the 3rd note in the major chord (E in the case above) makes the chord sound happy, whereas the flattened third note in the minor chord (E♭ in the case above) makes the chord sound sad.

'PHEW!' IF ALL THAT INFO HAS YOUR BRAIN PUMPING BUT YOU STILL DON'T QUITE GET IT, DON'T WORRY. AS WITH A LOT OF THINGS ON THE GUITAR, THEY BECOME CLEARER AS MORE PIECES OF THE PUZZLE COME TOGETHER. THIS BRIEF EXPLANATION WILL BE ENOUGH TO KEEP YOU GOING FOR NOW. WE ARE READY TO UNDERSTAND POWER CHORDS!

HOW TO PLAY POWER CHORDS

Power chords differ from major and minor chords in one very crucial way: they have no 3rd. Remember how we described the 3rd note in the major chord as sounding happy and the flat 3rd in the minor chord as sounding sad? Well, the power chord has neither. It simply has the 1st and the 5th notes in it from the major scale. There are two reasons why we need to know this.

1 WHERE TO USE THE CHORD

As the chord is neither major nor minor it can be used for both! So if you are covering a song with a C major and E minor chord in it, you could make it more 'rock' by just using a C power chord and an A power chord.

2 HOW IT WORKS WITH GAIN

When you add distortion to the major or minor chords to create a rock, metal or punk sound, it will be muffled because the open chords have so many notes. When you use the two-note power chords, you get a much crisper-sounding rock chord!

If you want to hear how these two chords should sound, go online and click on **Skill 6 – Power chords.**

POSITION 1 POWER CHORDS

A5 POSITION 1

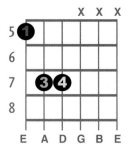

Power chords are known as 5th chords. This is because the chord only consists of the first and fifth note from the scale. So this first chord we are attempting is called A5.

FRONT VIEW

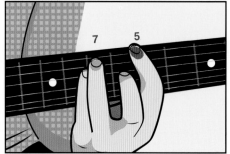

SIDE VIEW 1

SIDE VIEW 2

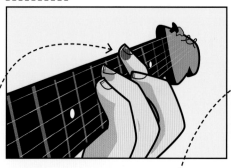

PLAYER'S VIEW

Your 1st finger should start on the 5th fret. Why? Well that's because we are playing an A power chord and the 5th fret of the E string is where the A-note is. We will talk about this more on the next page.

Notice the 1st finger is flat against all six strings. This is ok because we are deliberately trying to block the G, B and E string. You don't need to push the finger down, just rest it on the strings.

POSITION 2 POWER CHORDS

D5 POSITION 2

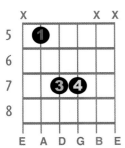

The difference between Position 1 and Position 2 power chords is that Position 1 starts on the E string and Position 2 starts on the A string. As you can see here, your 1st finger is on the 5th fret of the A string. The 5th fret on the A string is D. Therefore this is a D5.

FRONT VIEW

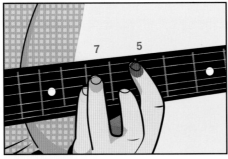

SIDE VIEW 1

SIDE VIEW 2

PLAYER'S VIEW

YOUR FIRST TASK

Before we move on, spend some time trying to play both the A5 and the D5 power chords. Here is a checklist to consider when playing these chords:

1 THREE STRINGS CLEAR
Make sure that you hear the strings you are pushing down nice and clearly. They may need to be pushed down very hard to make the correct sound.

2 MUTED STRINGS
The rest of the strings should be muted. This means that your 1st finger just rests on the strings that aren't being played. This will 'deaden' the sound and stop them ringing out.

3 LOW E STRING MUTE
To mute the E string for the Position 2 chords, you simply need to touch it with the very tip of your 1st finger (see the 'player's view' above). This will stop the string from ringing out.

BRINGING THE ROCK!

These power chords sound best when played through an electric guitar with a bit of gain! So if you have an amp and an electric guitar, plug it in, dial up the gain knob all the way (you may want to turn down the volume at the same time) and try to strum these power chords. The whole point behind muting the remaining strings is that you are able to strum all six strings and only hear the three fretted notes. This should be extremely effective when you plug in through an amp. Give it a go if you can!

QUICK TIP
Gain is the sound you get when you push the valves in your guitar amp to the limit! The sound is grittier and more distorted than the clean sound of the amp before you turn the gain up.

EVERY SINGLE POWER CHORD

Now that you can play the two positions of the power chord, you can play every single power chord! It's simple. The power chord shape is exactly the same everywhere on the guitar. The only thing that changes is where you put the chord. Here is an example.

The 1st finger is on the 5th fret (which is A), therefore this is an A5.

This shows the same shape as before, except now the 1st finger is on the 3rd fret (which is G). Therefore this is a G5.

POSITION 1 A5

POSITION 1 G5

The 1st finger is on the 5th fret of the A string (which is D), therefore this is a D5.

This is the same shape as before, except now the 1st finger is on the 3rd fret (which is C). Therefore this is a C5.

POSITION 2 D5

POSITION 2 C5

NOTES ON THE A STRING

We have learned the notes on the E string, but to play the Position 2 power chords, you need to know the notes on the A string too, so here they are!

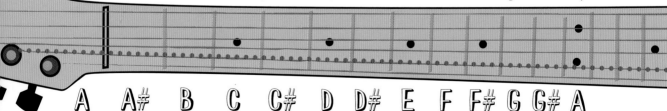

A   A#   B   C   C#   D   D#   E   F   F#   G   G#   A

LET'S RIFF!

To practise these power chords, we will be learning a cool rock riff!

Your first task is to listen to the riff, so go online and click on **Skill 6 – Powerchord Riff**. Remember, this riff is played with a lot of distortion on the guitar, so for it to sound exactly the same when you play, you need gain!

Step 1: THE CHORD CHART

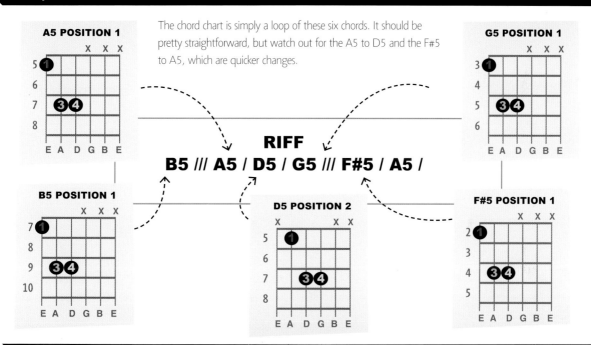

The chord chart is simply a loop of these six chords. It should be pretty straightforward, but watch out for the A5 to D5 and the F#5 to A5, which are quicker changes.

RIFF

B5 /// A5 / D5 / G5 /// F#5 / A5 /

Step 2: THE RHYTHM

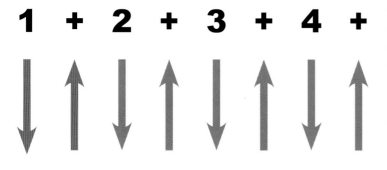

1 + 2 + 3 + 4 +

The riff has a simple rhythm pattern to allow you to focus on the chord changes. The only complication is that as soon as you have strummed the two arrows, you need to stop the chord ringing. You do this by releasing the pressure on the chord (that is, don't push down anymore!). On the last two chords (F#5 and A5), you simply do a single strum and you hold the pressure on for the whole bar.

PENTATONIC MAGIC

It's now time for you to learn something called the pentatonic scale. This scale is the backbone to blues, rock, jazz, soul, pop, gospel and many more styles. Every time you listen to your favourite rock riffs, blues solos or soul melodies, you are listening to the pentatonic scale in some form.

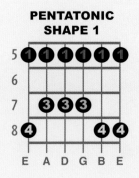

PENTATONIC SHAPE 1

OUR FIRST PENTATONIC SHAPE

Here is the first pentatonic shape you will be learning. You read this diagram in the same way you would a chord chart (the horizontal lines are frets, the vertical lines are strings, and so on), with one fundamental difference. This is a scale chart, which means that you play each note separately. In a chord diagram, you try to put all your fingers on at once; in a scale diagram, you put each finger on separately. You read the diagram from left to right, and from string to string. So, in this instance, we play 5th fret E string first, followed by 8th fret E string. We then move on to 5th fret A string, followed by 7th fret A string. This is shown in the tab below.

PENTATONIC TAB

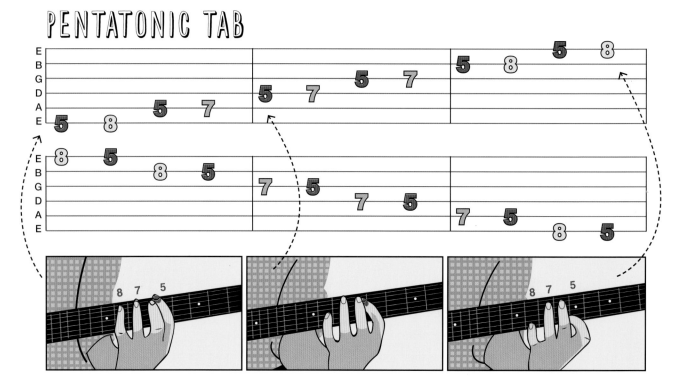

These diagrams help you see how your hand should look at certain points of the tab. Notice that your thumb should be at the back of the neck and remember which fingers you use for each colour on the tab.

Step 1: GETTING THE TECHNIQUE RIGHT

Your first task is to memorise this shape and get the technique correct.
Here are some tips to help you get it together quickly and efficiently.

1 ALTERNATE PICKING
Just as we did in Skill 2, we need to use alternate picking: downstroke on the first note, upstroke on second, down on third, and so on.

2 KEEP FINGERS CLOSE TO THE FRETBOARD
As you walk your fingers through the scale shape, try not to let them lift too far from the fretboard. The 1st finger in this picture shows the highest you need to go.

3 LITTLE FINGER POSITION
Use your little finger to stabilise your picking hand position. Simply lean the finger on the scratch plate. This allows you to do quicker and more accurate movements with your wrist when you pick.

4 THUMB AT THE BACK OF NECK
As we discussed in Skill 2, keep your thumb flat on the back of the neck. You should be a little more used to this by now, but keep checking it. Don't let it creep out of position!

Step 2: TRAINING THE SHAPE

When you are happy with your hand position and comfortable with the technique of playing the shape, it is time to put in some repetitive practice! Play through the entire shape and then start again, and just keep looping the shape as long as you can. Get your metronome out and try it with a beat as well.

QUICK TIP
Focus on your fretting hand (left hand) not your picking hand. Trust your picking hand to keep up with your left hand. If you have been practising those spider exercises, then it will keep up!

Playing the shape with a drum loop or metronome is an important part of learning it. Online, you can listen to three audio files of the pentatonic shape being played at three different speeds. Each track lasts for 5 minutes, so you can use them as warm-ups. Click on:
Skill 7 – Pentatonic Scale 50 BPM • Skill 7 – Pentatonic Scale 70 BPM • Skill 7 – Pentatonic Scale 90 BPM

MOVING INTO DIFFERENT KEYS

Now that you have learnt the scale shape and are starting to play it reasonably well, it is time to explain how you can start using this scale shape to make music. You may have heard music people bandy the term 'key' around before. The key of a song is its tonal centre – the basic underlying note of the song. For example, you can have a song in the key of C major. This means that its tonal centre is C major. No matter what other chords it uses, it will always sound like you have resolved (completed) the song when you play the C.

OK... SO HOW DOES THIS HELP ME?!

Knowing the key of a song or backing track will enable you to improvise (or solo) over it. You will be able to take the scale shape, put it into the correct key and then play *any* of the notes in the scale and it will sound good over the track. The examples below will help to make this clearer.

Example 1: THE KEY OF A MINOR

1 YOU ARE GIVEN THE KEY We have this backing track in the key of A minor. So, we need to take our pentatonic shape and put it into this key so that we can improvise and solo using it.

Put these ideas to the test by playing along to the backing track. Click on **Skill 7 – Backing Track (A Minor key)**.

2 MOVE YOUR PENTATONIC SHAPE TO START ON A We take our 1st finger, place it on A (on the E string) and start playing the shape.

3 PLAY ANY NOTE! Once our shape is in position you can play any note in any order and it will 'work' over the track. This is what it means to be playing in the correct key.

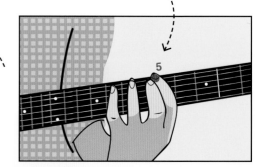

SOUND TOO SIMPLE?

That's because it is that simple! You are told the key, you put your 1st finger on the note of the key (wherever it is on the E string) and then play the pentatonic shape. Voilà!

Example 2: THE KEY OF G MINOR

1 YOU ARE GIVEN THE KEY
Now you are told to play in the key of G minor. Not a problem at all. You'll be improvising and making sweet, sweet music in no time.

Put these ideas to the test by playing along to the backing track. Click on **Skill 7 – Backing Track (G Minor key)**.

2 MOVE YOUR PENTATONIC SHAPE TO START ON G
Place your 1st finger on G (3rd fret on the E string) and start playing the shape.

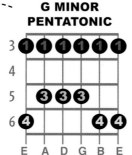

G MINOR PENTATONIC

3 PLAY ANY NOTE!
Once your shape is in position, you can play any note in any order.

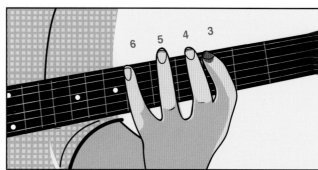

Example 3: THE KEY OF B MINOR

1 YOU ARE GIVEN THE KEY
Now you are told to play in the key of B minor.

Put these ideas to the test by playing along to the backing track. Click on **Skill 7 – Backing Track (B Minor key)**.

2 MOVE YOUR PENTATONIC SHAPE TO START ON B
Place your 1st finger on B (7th fret on the E string) and start playing the shape.

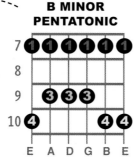

B MINOR PENTATONIC

3 PLAY ANY NOTE!
You can now play any note in any order and it will 'work' over the track. You have successfully moved to the key of B minor.

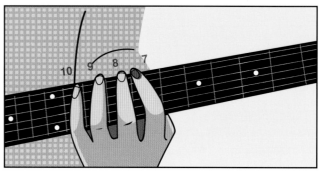

And there we have it! You can now change keys. Practice changing to these three keys and play the scale over the backing tracks provided to hear what it sounds like.

NOTE: This method is only for minor keys. We will tackle major keys later on in the book.

PENTATONIC EXERCISES

A great way to really get to know the pentatonic shape inside out is to practise what we call 'sequences'. The idea behind these sequences is that you are playing a repeating pattern as you move through the shape. Sequences are not only great for improving alternate picking and finger speed, they are also extremely useable patterns when it comes to improvising and soloing. Here are two exercises to practise.

Exercise 1: 3 UP, 1 DOWN

With any sequence, we are looking for the pattern. In this instance, we play the notes on the E, A and D strings (six notes). We then go back one string (back to A) and play another three strings from there. See the dotted lines on the tab for where the sequence repeats.

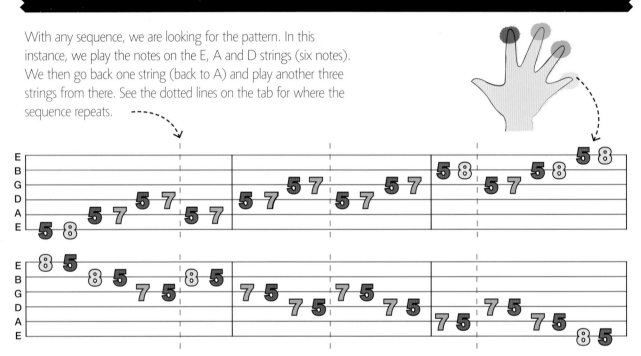

SAME SHAPE, NEW ORDER!

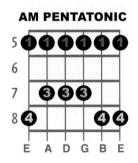

AM PENTATONIC

Apart from learning a new order to play the notes in, you are still using exactly the same shape you've already learnt. The exercise is tabbed out in the key of A minor. So you are using the A minor pentatonic shape. Once you have worked out the sequence, you can easily move it into any other key. Try playing the sequence in B minor. It's exactly the same except you'll be starting on the 7th fret and playing through the shape from there.

AND DON'T FORGET...

1. KEEP FINGERS CLOSE TO THE FRETBOARD
2. USE ALTERNATE PICKING
3. THUMB AT THE BACK OF THE NECK

Exercise 2: STRING SKIPPING

This second sequence is all about learning how to skip strings. The basic idea is that you play one string, then skip a string, then return to the string you have skipped and start again from there. The bar line in this tab shows you the sequence divide line.

The key to playing this exercise correctly is your picking hand. You may need to spend some time getting used to jumping between strings, but as long as you continue to use **alternate picking** for every note, you will eventually get there!

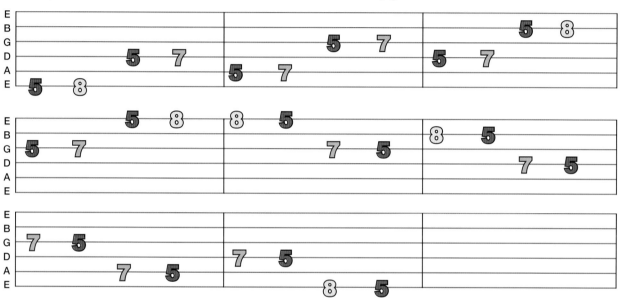

Both of these exercises have been recorded at a relatively slow pace so that you can have a listen to how they should sound. Don't forget to get your metronome out to practise them!
Skill 7 – Exercise 1 (3 Up, 1 Down)   Skill 7 – Exercise 2 (String Skipping)

BEFORE THE NEXT STEP

In the next chapter we will be using the pentatonic scale as well as your power chords and open chords to put together a really challenging modern rock song. Follow this practice routine to help ensure you have a good grasp of this pentatonic scale and the ways to move it into different keys.

1 WARM-UPS

Start with your two spider exercises, followed by two pentatonic scale exercises. These should be played with a metronome or drum loop, and you should continue to monitor your speed in BPM.

2 OPEN CHORD SONG

Play through the open chord song a few times round to ensure those chords are still sounding great!

3 POWER CHORD RIFF

Play through the riff you learnt in the previous lesson (go through it 2 to 3 times) to ensure you are making more progress with your power chords.

4 IMPROVISING

Get those backing tracks on (as discussed on page 45) and start playing over them with your pentatonic scales.

BE A MODERN-DAY GUITARIST

In this chapter we will apply everything we have learnt so far by learning how to play a full-blown song! This song consists of a pentatonic lead riff and a power chord section, as well as strumming and the open chords. It has everything you expect a modern-day guitarist to play in one song.

Your first job is as easy as it gets – just listen! Click on the link to **Skill 8 – Main Song** and listen to the whole thing. As you listen, think to yourself, 'When I finish this chapter, I'll be able to play this song!'

BEFORE WE START...

Before we start looking at the song, let's clarify one guitar myth that needs addressing: what is the modern-day guitarist? There was a time when the notion of playing either a rhythm or a lead guitar was very popular. These days, the best guitarists do both equally well. So, with this song we lose the idea of one or the other and combine the two aspects.

LEAD GUITARIST?

RHYTHM GUITARIST?

Step 1: THE CHORD CHART

Let's begin with the chord chart for the song. Remember, the chord chart is the outline of the song and does not include any more information than what chords are played and for how long.

INTRO (RIFF)

Am /// C /// D /// F /// Am /// C /// D /// F /// Am (///)

VERSE ONE

Am /// F /// C /// G /// Am /// F /// C /// G ///
Am /// F /// C /// G /// Am /// F /// C /// G ///
F /// /// D /// ///

CHORUS ONE

Am /// C /// G /// D /// Am /// C /// G /// D ///
Am /// C /// G /// D /// Am /// C /// G /// D ///

RE-INTRO (RIFF)

Am /// C /// D /// F /// Am /// C /// D /// F /// Am (///)

VERSE TWO

Am /// F /// C /// G /// Am /// F /// C /// G ///
Am /// F /// C /// G /// Am /// F /// C /// G ///
F /// /// D /// ///

CHORUS TWO

Am /// C /// G /// D /// Am /// C /// G /// D ///
Am /// C /// G /// D /// Am /// C /// G /// D ///

RE-INTRO (RIFF)

Am /// C /// D /// F /// Am /// C /// D /// F /// Am (///)

OUTRO (FADE OUT)

Am /// F /// C /// G /// Am /// F /// C /// G ///
Am /// F /// C /// G /// Am /// F /// C /// G ///

THE A MINOR CHORD

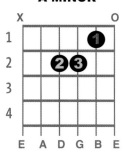

A MINOR

FRONT VIEW

The first new chord is relatively easy. A quick tip is to play an E major chord and move the whole shape down one string. Spend a few minutes getting to grips with this chord and the way it sounds before attempting the F Major.

PLAYER'S VIEW

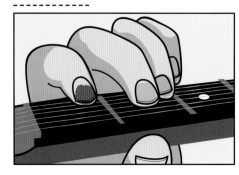

SIDE VIEW 1

THE F MAJOR CHORD

F MAJOR

FRONT VIEW

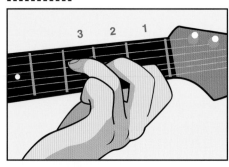

SIDE VIEW

PLAYER'S VIEW

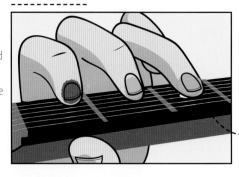

There are a lot of ways to play the F major chord, but to start with we will play it as it is shown here. The main notes of the chord are the three you are pushing down, but it is OK for now to use the open A string and E string.

Notice how the joint at the top of the finger is totally bent. This allows you to create a bridge with the fingers even with the big finger stretch that we have in this chord.

The fingers are all at the edge of the frets for a clear sound, and the fingertips are digging into the strings to allow that bridge (as explained above).

Step 2: THE STRUMMING PATTERN

The next step is to add the strumming to the chord progression. The pattern we are using is the universal strumming pattern. By now you should have this pattern pretty well learnt, so it is just a case of getting used to the chord changes.

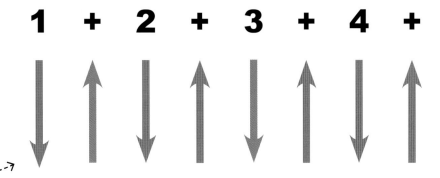

We have a version of the song that is only the acoustic chords strummed for you to play along with. The vocals are still there, but no lead guitar. This will allow you to focus on the acoustic playing. This is also ideal for those of you who only have an acoustic guitar. Click on **Skill 8 – Acoustic Version.**

Step 3: THE POWER CHORDS

We are now adding power chords to the verse, which you will play instead of the open chords. The first line is still open chords, so continue to play them. As soon as you get to the second line, you play power chords.

VERSE

Am /// **F** /// **C** /// **G** /// **Am** /// **F** /// **C** /// **G** ///
A5 /// **F5** /// **C5** /// **G5** /// **A5** /// **F5** /// **C5** /// **G5** ///
F5 /// /// **D5** /// ///

We now get to the power chords instead of the open chords. We only strum each power chord on the first beat of each bar ('Strum , 2, 3, 4...'). This allows the distortion to ring out. Try to find these chords before they are revealed on the next page!

FEEL THE POWER

THE POWER CHORD POSITIONS

If you haven't worked them out already, here are the five power chords you need to play.

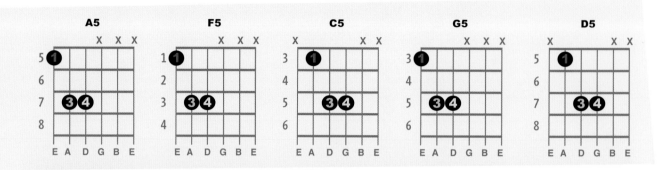

Step 4: PENTATONIC LEAD RIFF

The intro guitar riff is tabbed out in full below. You should be at a point where you fully understand how to use the tab, so try to get what you see on this page to sound like the riff on the track!

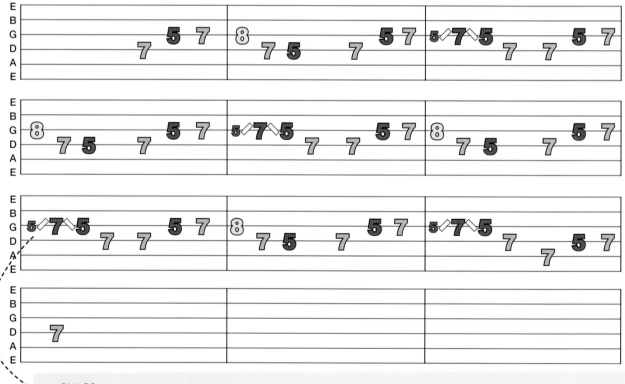

SLIDES

This white diagonal line is a slide. This means you put your 1st finger on the 5th fret and then slide it up to the 7th fret, and then back down to the 5th fret. Keep your finger pushed down against the fretboard the entire time, nice and hard. It may take a bit of practice, but it sounds super cool when you get it together!

Step 5: PUTTING IT ALL TOGETHER

It's time to put the whole thing together. To do so, we will be using a slower version of the song that you can find by clicking on the link to **Skill 8 – Slow Version**.
There is also a version with no vocals. Go to **Skill 8 – No Vocals**.

RIFF FOR THE INTRO

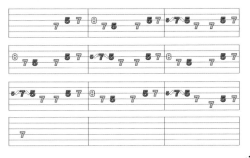

VERSES

You play the first half of the verse using your open chords and the strumming pattern, then you move to power chords for the second half of the verse.

CHORUSES

The choruses are entirely open chords with the universal strumming pattern. As soon as you finish the last chord of the chorus, return to the intro riff (which means you have to jump up to the pentatonic shape very quickly!).

OUTRO

This is all open chords with the universal strumming pattern. The track gradually fades out to silence, so just play until the track is totally silent.

INTRO (RIFF)
Am /// **C** /// **D** /// **F** /// **Am** /// **C** /// **D** /// **F** /// **Am** (///)

VERSE ONE
Am /// **F** /// **C** /// **G** /// **Am** /// **F** /// **C** /// **G** ///
Am /// **F** /// **C** /// **G** /// **Am** /// **F** /// **C** /// **G** ///
F /// /// **D** /// ///

CHORUS ONE
Am /// **C** /// **G** /// **D** /// **Am** /// **C** /// **G** /// **D** ///
Am /// **C** /// **G** /// **D** /// **Am** /// **C** /// **G** /// **D** ///

RE-INTRO (RIFF)
Am /// **C** /// **D** /// **F** /// **Am** /// **C** /// **D** /// **F** /// **Am** (///)

VERSE TWO
Am /// **F** /// **C** /// **G** /// **Am** /// **F** /// **C** /// **G** ///
Am /// **F** /// **C** /// **G** /// **Am** /// **F** /// **C** /// **G** ///
F /// /// **D** /// ///

CHORUS TWO
Am /// **C** /// **G** /// **D** /// **Am** /// **C** /// **G** /// **D** ///
Am /// **C** /// **G** /// **D** /// **Am** /// **C** /// **G** /// **D** ///

RE-INTRO (RIFF)
Am /// **C** /// **D** /// **F** /// **Am** /// **C** /// **D** /// **F** /// **Am** (///)

OUTRO (FADE OUT)
Am /// **F** /// **C** /// **G** /// **Am** /// **F** /// **C** /// **G** ///
Am /// **F** /// **C** /// **G** /// **Am** /// **F** /// **C** /// **G** ///

DONE!
AND THAT'S IT! DO YOUR BEST TO PUT IT ALL TOGETHER TO THE SLOWER TRACK AND ONLY THEN ATTEMPT THE FULL-PACE ONE. WHEN YOU CAN PLAY IT, MOVE ON TO THE NEXT SKILL!

CONQUERING CHORDS

In this chapter there is a selection of new chord shapes to learn. The theme is creativity, as we start to delve into 'fancier' chords that will open up a whole new world of sounds to play. We will be looking at bluesy chords, jazzy chords and even funky chords. At the end of the chapter we will talk about how you can start writing your own songs, so be sure to put your creative hat on!

CHORD RECAP!

Let's begin by quickly going over all the chords we have learnt so far in this book. Play through this chord chart. Just one strum on each chord will do, as this is simply a test of your memory. If there are any you can't remember, go back to the chapters where we covered them to remind yourself.

Asus2 /// **Cmaj7** /// **Em** /// **Am** /// **D** /// **G** ///
G /// **E** /// **A** /// **F** ///

THE D MINOR CHORD

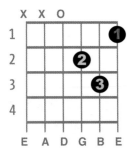

D MINOR

X X O
E A D G B E

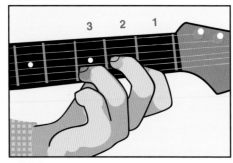

FRONT VIEW

SIDE VIEW 1

SIDE VIEW 2

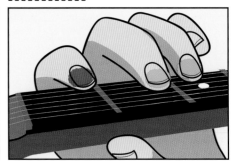

PLAYER'S VIEW

We have one final basic chord to add to the pile, and that is the D minor chord. This is a tricky little shape to get right. The key note is the 1st fret of the E string. This is the flat third (see Skill 6, page 36 for the theory), so make sure it's ringing out clearly.

FUNKY & JAZZY CHORDS

The more technical name for funky or jazzy chords are 7th chords. There are three types of 7th chords: major 7th, minor 7th and dominant 7th. Each has a unique sound. For the moment, we will be looking at the open chord versions of some of them as they will add some spice to your chord playing. Let's have a look at major 7th and minor 7th chords.

MAJOR 7TH CHORDS

Amaj7

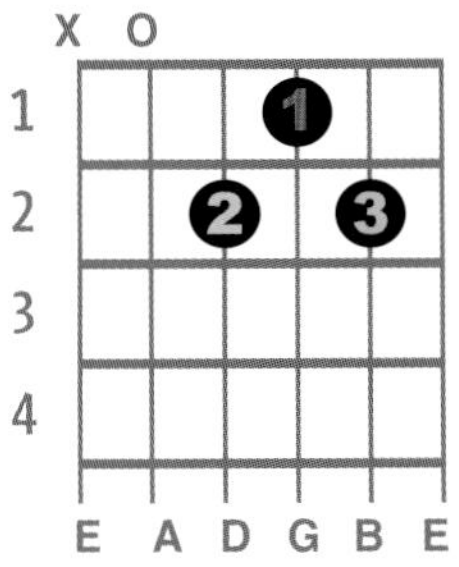

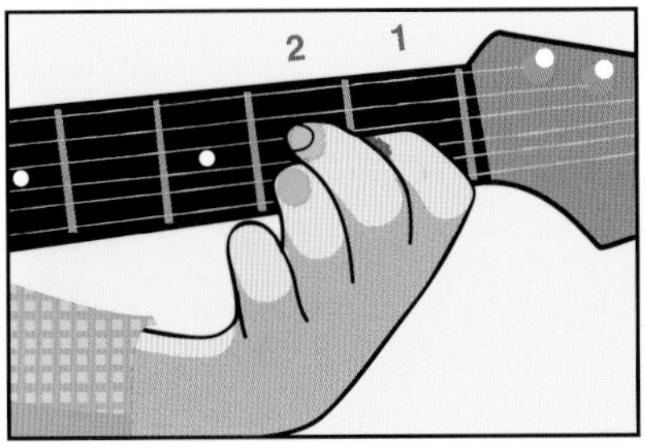

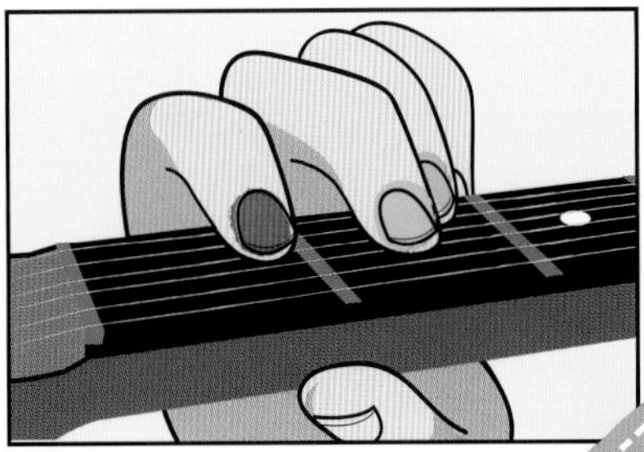

Dmaj7

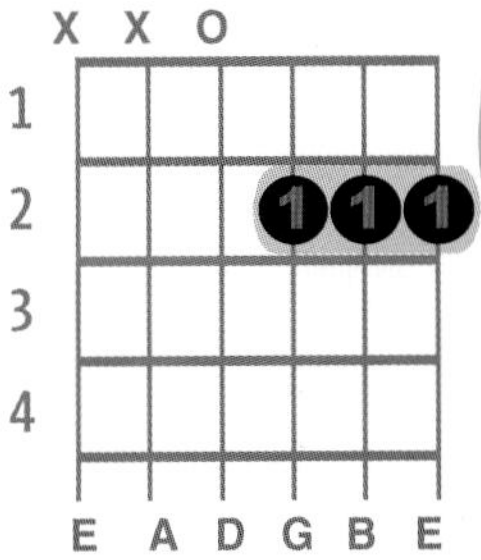

SOUND
You need to use your own ears at this point to try and remember the sounds of these chords. They can sound really chilled and jazzy!

MINOR 7TH CHORDS

Am7

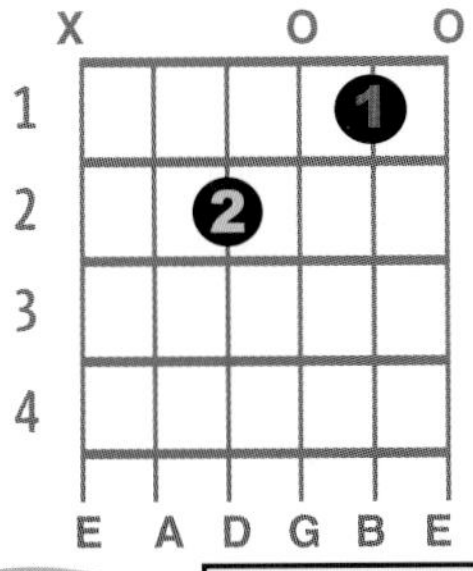

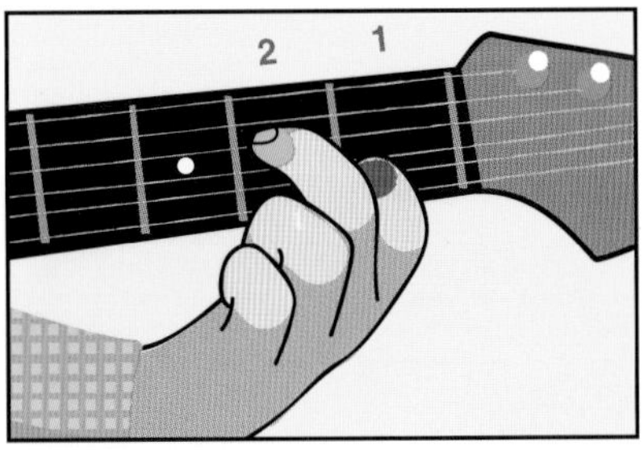

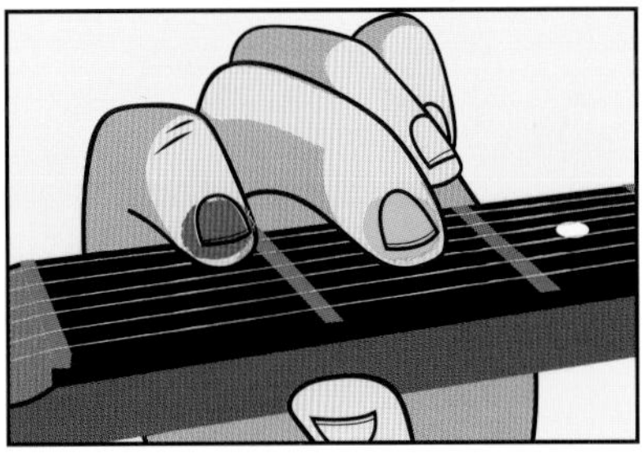

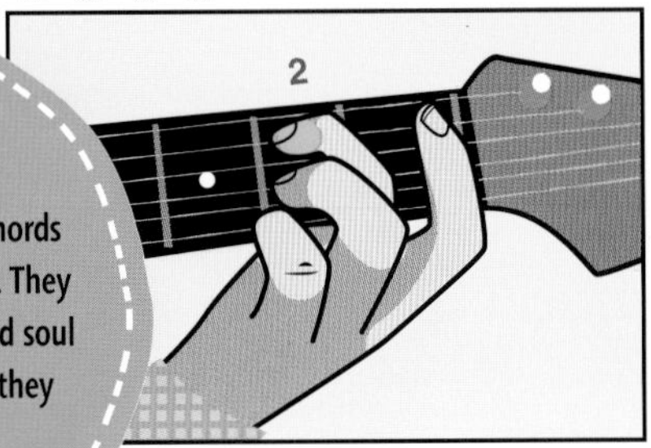

Em7

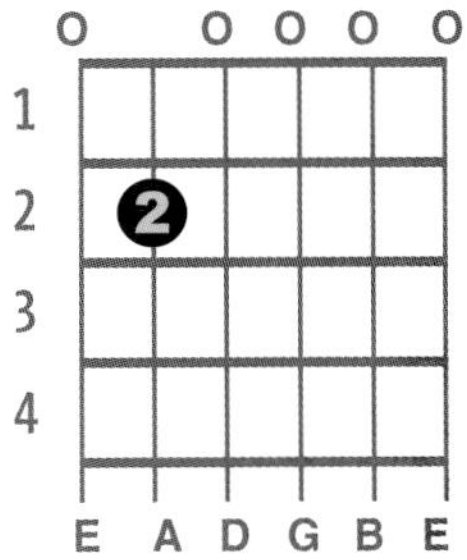

SOUND
These are basically minor chords with a more chilled-out feel. They are common in jazz, funk and soul music. What do you think they sound like?

BLUESY CHORDS

Dominant 7th chords have a special place in blues music because they sound particularly unresolved. This means that when you play these chords it really sounds as though you need to play something else at the end – a nice major or minor chord to resolve the sound. This feel is perfect because the blues are all about tension and release. Give these three chord shapes a try.

Listen to all the chords from this chapter to check you are playing them correctly. Click on **Skill 9 – Chords**.

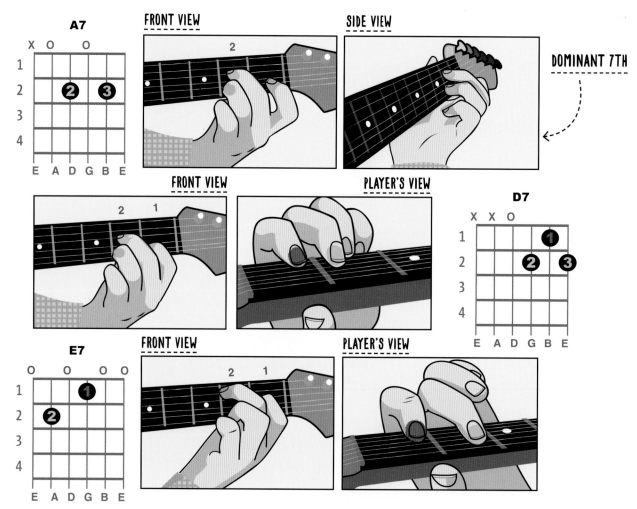

THERE ARE A LOT OF CHORDS OUT THERE...

... but you can generally group chords into three different types – major, minor and dominant. As with every rule, there are exceptions but, for the moment, you can think of most chords as being in these categories. Major chords have the happiest, most chilled sound. Minor chords have a slightly darker sound and the dominant chords have that unresolved sound. Thinking of chords in this way is important when writing music, so be sure to use your ears as you're learning them!

LET'S GET CREATIVE!

To write a song, you need to put a chord chart together, choose a rhythm and then maybe add a lead line or some vocals over the top. Sounds simple when put like that and, fundamentally, it is! If you've made it this far, you've already learnt a lot. We are now going to start your song-writing career right here with a rough song-writing guide.

BEFORE YOU START, ASK YOURSELF SOME QUESTIONS

To get those creative juices flowing, ask yourself a few questions whilst you're writing this song. 'What kind of song is this? Is it upbeat and quick, slow and chilled or somewhere in the middle?' 'Am I writing in a particular style – rock, or blues or folk – or am I just seeing what happens?' The answers to these questions will really help you zone in on the song. For example, if you answered the first question by saying you want an upbeat song, this will affect the type of rhythm pattern you want to play. If you answered the second question by saying you want a bluesy song, you may want to focus on the dominant 7th, bluesy chords.

1 PICK FOUR CHORDS

Pick four chords from the new selection we just learnt. Don't just pick randomly – try a few combinations and decide which ones you like the sound of. These will be your verse chords. Once you have decided, make sure you can play them clearly and move to Step 2.

? /// ? /// ? /// ? ///

2 CHOOSE A RHYTHM PATTERN

Until now we've been using the universal rhythm pattern for most songs. This time, create your own rhythm pattern! Below is the blank rhythm pattern. All you need to do is colour some arrows red. Never forget the fundamentals of rhythm patterns – keep your arm moving at all times!

1 + 2 + 3 + 4 +

3 PICK FOUR MORE CHORDS

Create a chorus with four more chords. Think about the chords you have already used, and try to vary it a little. Also, if you are starting to develop a theme (maybe the song is sounding very jazzy, for example), try to pick chords that fit in with the previous ones. You are using nothing more than your ears at this stage... and you can't get it wrong. This is your own composition; you simply cannot get it wrong!

? /// ? /// ? /// ? ///

4 CHOOSE A NEW RHYTHM PATTERN

For the chorus, we want to mix it up a bit. Choose a new rhythm pattern with the four chorus chords. It doesn't have to be drastically different, but it can be if you want. You may want to add more arrows to make the chorus sound more intense than the verse, but it's up to you!

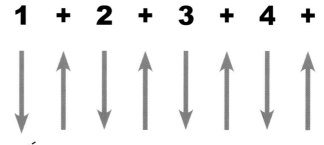

1 + 2 + 3 + 4 +

5 HAVE SOME FUN!

This is a fun process that has no barriers other than those of your own imagination. These steps will get you started, but there are no rules. Anything you do will be your very own creation. There is no right or wrong, just opinions. If you like it and enjoy writing the song, then it is a great song! Have a bit of fun getting all these chords learnt and writing a few songs. Then we'll head on to the next chapter.

IMPROVISING WITH LEAD

Some of the biggest thrills of learning and playing the guitar are being able to improvise a killer guitar solo, writing an amazing guitar riff or melody, and learning how to play awesome songs. Well, we now know how to learn songs: we use tab, chord charts and our ears. We've learnt some cool riffs to get started on the road to writing the next big hit. So there is only really one aspect left to cover – solos! This is very much an electric guitar concept, but there is a lot in this chapter that can be done on the acoustic guitar. It will improve your general playing as well, so read on!

LEAD GUITAR TECHNIQUES

To take your lead playing to the next level, you need to learn three new techniques:

1 BENDS   **2** SLIDES   **3** HAMMER-ONS

Step 1: GUITAR BENDS

To do a full bend, you bend the string up a whole tone, as if you had played a note two notes above the fretted note).

Choose any note on the G string (in this example, we are using the 7th fret G string) and play it with the 3rd finger. Be sure that you also have your 2nd finger pushed down on the fret before (6th) and 1st finger pushed down on the fret before that (5th). This is your hand position before you bend.

When you have the hand position correct, push down all three fingers very hard and push them upwards to bend the string. The common mistakes people make are not pushing down hard enough (the note will stop sounding) and letting the string slip under the finger. As long as you are pushing down hard, you can avoid these errors.

QUICK TIP

In these pictures, the thumb is placed over the top of the neck. However, you can perform the bend just as confidently with the thumb flat on the back of the neck. Do whichever feels the most comfortable to you.

MORE ON BENDS

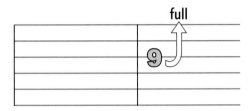

This is how you tab out a bend. The '9' refers to the fret you are holding, and the upwards arrow tells you to bend it up. At the top of the arrow there will be an instruction. In this case, 'full' means do the bend we practised on the previous page (bend up two frets).

If you are unsure as to which note the bend should sound like, follow these steps.

1 PLAY THE NOTE YOU ARE BENDING TO
If you are doing as this tab says and bending the 9th fret G string, the first thing you should do is play the 11th fret (two frets up). This is the note you should be trying to hit.

2 RETURN TO THE 9TH AND BEND!
Quickly return to the 9th fret and bend it whilst you still have the sound of the other note in your head. You'll soon be able to hear if you are getting close. This is a great exercise for your ear as well.

Step 2: GUITAR SLIDES

Slides are a lot easier than bends. As we have already played a slide on the guitar (back in Skill 8 for the riff), we will cover it briefly here.

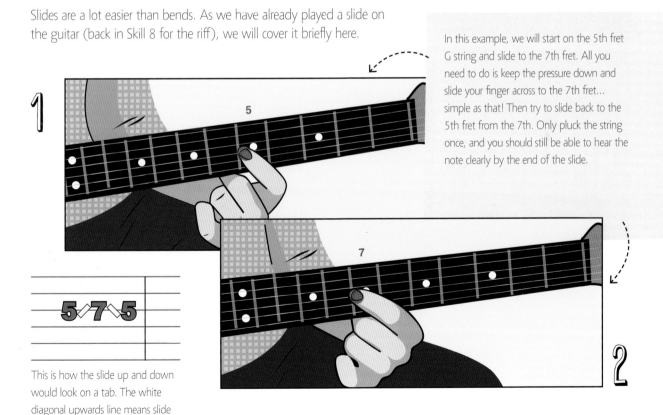

In this example, we will start on the 5th fret G string and slide to the 7th fret. All you need to do is keep the pressure down and slide your finger across to the 7th fret... simple as that! Then try to slide back to the 5th fret from the 7th. Only pluck the string once, and you should still be able to hear the note clearly by the end of the slide.

This is how the slide up and down would look on a tab. The white diagonal upwards line means slide up, and the opposite is slide down.

Step 3: HAMMER-ONS & PULL-OFFS

This is an important technique that is also called legato playing (very smooth playing) because you are using the plectrum less and the fretting hand more. A hammer-on is basically holding one note and then using another finger to push on the next note (without plucking it). Let's look at it in more detail.

Start by holding the 5th fret of the G string with your 1st finger. You need to play this note clearly and make sure your 3rd finger is ready to move.

As soon as you've played the 5th fret, throw your 3rd finger down onto the 7th fret. You need to do it accurately and with some force to get the note to sound. It will sound faint at first. Eventually, you will be able to get it to the same volume as the picked note. This is a hammer-on.

QUICK TIP
You don't need to lift your 1st finger up when you hammer on. This isn't like a see-saw – just because the 3rd finger goes down, the 1st doesn't have to come up! Keep that finger down on the 5th fret.

PULL-OFFS

The pull-off is the reverse action of the hammer-on. You start with your 3rd finger on the 7th fret (whilst holding your 1st finger on the 5th fret) and pull away the 3rd finger to reveal the 1st finger, thus pulling off the note. The secret here is to pluck the string with your 3rd finger. In the second picture it looks like that 3rd finger has been pulled downwards. That's because the string has been plucked using a downwards motion. It takes some practice, but you'll get it!

This is how you show a hammer-on or pull-off on a piece of tab (the curved line). In the first part we see that we hammer on from the 7th fret to the 9th. In the next bit we hammer on from 7th to 9th, then pull off back to 7th. So it's the same curved line for hammering on and pulling off, but if the frets go up you're hammering on, if they go down you're pulling off. Simple!

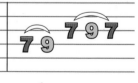

PENTATONIC SHAPE 2

In Skill 7 we learnt how to play a shape in the pentatonic scale. There are in fact five shapes to learn, and today we will focus on shape two. The idea is that eventually you will be able to play the scale across the whole neck, allowing you to improvise freely across the whole guitar.

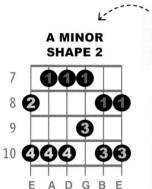

A MINOR SHAPE 2

Here is your second shape. Your first step is to try and memorise it. Pay close attention to the fingers you should be using on each note.

It is important to understand how this shape relates to the first. In this diagram, you should be able to see Shape 1 and 2 and how they overlap. Play Shape 1 and then Shape 2 in A minor, and try to see how the two overlap. This is crucial when we come to the solo at the end of this skill level.

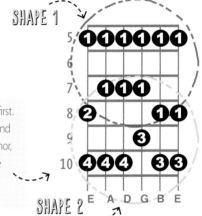

USING THE TWO SHAPES

Remember how we talked about improvising using the pentatonic Shape 1 in any minor key? If you have been practising, you should be starting to understand it a little more. Now we have Shape 2; not only can we do minor keys, but we can very easily approach major keys, too. Here's why…

THE FIRST NOTE IS THE MAJOR ROOT NOTE
We only need to understand this on a basic level for the moment, so just take this as gospel for now. The first note of Shape 2 is the major key root note (first note). In practice, this means that if you need to improvise in A major, you could put your 2nd finger on the A root note (5th fret) and play Shape 2 from there.

A MAJOR PENTATONIC (SHAPE 2)

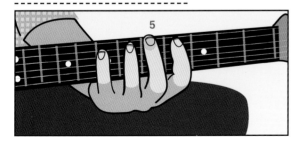

C MAJOR PENTATONIC (SHAPE 2)

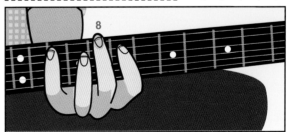

Put these ideas to the test by playing along to the backing tracks online. Click on the links to **Skill 10 – Backing Track (B Major)** and **Skill 10 – Backing Track (D Major)**

YOUR FIRST GUITAR SOLO

To help put all of these new techniques and the new scale shape into practice, you will learn a guitar solo!
This solo contains all the techniques we have discussed, uses pentatonic Shape 1 and Shape 2, and is written
in the key of B minor. All in all, it's a pretty cool challenge and something to seriously get your teeth into!

First, you just need to listen. Click on the link to **Skill 10 – Guitar Solo.** The first 30 seconds or so is the intro of the track, then the solo kicks in and repeats until the end. Listen until you can hum the solo, then check out the tab below. You can also play along to the slower version, until you get the hang of it.

THE SOLO TAB

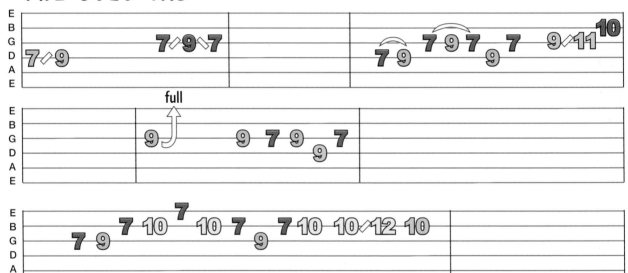

USEFUL TIPS

1 LEARN BAR BY BAR
When tackling a whole solo like this, the best approach is to learn a bar at a time. Learn the first bar until you can play it well and have it memorised, then move on to the next.

2 PIECE IT TOGETHER
Once you have learnt bars 1 and 2, try to piece them together in time. When you can do that, move on to the next bar and continue the same gradual process.

3 KEEP LISTENING
The worst thing you can do is lose focus about what this solo should sound like. With every single bar you learn, you should try to get it sounding like the track before moving on.

4 SPOT THE SHAPES
Don't learn this like a parrot! Be sure you can see the pentatonic shapes within what you are playing. The solo uses Shapes 1 and 2, so make sure you know when you play in each of those shapes.

A LOOK TO THE NEXT STEP

We have covered a huge amount of material over the last 10 chapters, but the great news is that this is just the beginning! The techniques and skills we have learnt will act as extremely solid foundations that you can continue to build on as you step into a more intermediate stage of guitar playing. Here is a quick summary of the things you should look into to continue to improve your guitar playing. Whether from a more advanced book, on-line courses or a guitar tutor near you, these are the things you will want to learn moer about.

THE NEXT STEP FOR AN ELECTRIC PLAYER

If you have found that you love the idea of soloing, playing riffs, power chords and big sounds that can only be achieved on an electric instrument, then here are a few pointers as to what to do next.

1 NEW RHYTHMS We deliberately used one main rhythm pattern in this book because we have enough on our plates learning all the new chords, scales and songs. However, now would be the time to take your rhythm playing up a gear. The best way to do this is to plunge right into new songs from various genres, as they will each have a different rhythm that you can learn.

2 BARRE CHORDS These are the next step in your chord playing and are a serious challenge. They will open up the neck even more and allow you to play a whole new world of cool songs.

3 THE FIVE PENTATONIC SHAPES We have looked at two pentatonic shapes, but you need all five to take your playing to the next level. There is so much you can do with these shapes, so they must be learnt. The improvisational aspect of the guitar should also be further explored. We have made a solid start, but improvising well takes hours of 'noodling' to discover things that work well. Learning licks within your scale shapes really helps, too.

4 THEORY We have covered as much theory as we have needed in this book but it is a very small fragment of fundamental guitar theory. To progress in your playing, you will need more in-depth knowledge. It will make you a better player because it will give you a deeper understanding of the instrument.

5 OTHER SCALES The pentatonic is not the only scale out there, and you need to learn your major and minor scales to be able to keep up with the theory as well as the riffs and solos you will tackle at an intermediate level.

QUICK TIP

You can divide your practice into four areas – rhythm playing, chords, lead and theory. This will allow you to tackle multiple areas at a time without really overdoing it. Choose a song with a new chord, new rhythm and a bit of lead. Try to play the whole thing. At the end of it, do you understand what you've played? That's where the theory kicks in. Applying this way of learning will guarantee your progress!

THE NEXT STEP FOR AN ACOUSTIC PLAYER

For pure acoustic players, the one difference to the list above would be to replace learning the five pentatonic shapes with learning fingerstyles. Fingerstyle is a technique of guitar playing without a plectrum. There are tonnes of ways you can approach fingerstyle playing, but one of the best places to start is by looking up something called Travis picking.

Having said all that, this book has already given you all the skills you need to play the guitar. As long as you have followed along with the skills and mastered each one before moving on, you can now strum, play some songs, write songs and even play a bit of lead guitar. This may be all that you set out to do, which is great! The guitar is an extremely rewarding and sociable instrument, so keep playing and keep having fun!